YOUTH MINISTRY

For Paul McGregor (1917-1976)
from whom I learned most
about ministry to youth

YOUTH MINISTRY

A Book of Readings

Edited by
Michael Warren

PAULIST PRESS
New York/Ramsey/Toronto

Library of Congress
Catalog Card Number: 77-70639

ISBN: 0-8091-2018-6

Published by Paulist Press
Editorial Office: 1865 Broadway, New York, N.Y. 10023
Business Office: 545 Island Road, Ramsey, N.J. 07446

Printed and bound in the
United States of America

ACKNOWLEDGEMENTS

We would like to express our gratitude to the indicated publishers for permission to reprint the following articles:

Alfonso M. Nebreda, S.J., "Faith and the Adolescent," *Teaching All Nations*, East Asian Pastoral Institute, Manila, Philippines, 11:3, 1974, pp. 141-160.

Alfonso M. Nebreda, S.J., "Education for Faith," *Good Tidings*, East Asian Pastoral Institute, Manila, Philippines, 12:5, 1973, pp. 225-228, 208.

Jose Calle, "Catholic Education as a Process of Evangelization," *Good Tidings*, East Asian Pastoral Institute, Manila, Philippines, 12:5, 1973, pp. 197-201.

Michael Warren, "Social Processes in Adolescent Catechesis," *The Living Light*, 9:4 (1972), Department of Education, United States Catholic Conference, Washington, D.C., pp. 77-88.

Thomas Zanzig, "The ACEC Experiment: A Multiple-Parish Approach to High School Religious Education (Part I)" and "The ACEC Experiment, Part Two: Initiating a Multiple-Parish Program for High School Religious Education," *PACE 6*, St. Mary's College Press, Winona, MN, 1975.

Michael Warren, "Christian Experience Weekends: Role of the Director" (original title: "Directing Christian Experience Weekends), *PACE 3*, St. Mary's College Press, Winona, MN, 1972.

"Reaching Out," Chapter 7 of *Five Cries of Youth* by Merton P. Strommen. Copyright © 1974 by Merton P. Strommen. By permission of Harper & Row, Publishers.

"Adolescent Girls: A Two-Year Study" is an interview with Gisela Konopka, who has developed this material in the recently published book, *Young Girls: A Portrait of Adolescence*, published by Prentice-Hall, Inc.

Michael Warren, "Resource Guide for Youth Ministry," *The Living Light*, 12:2 (1975), Department of Education, United States Catholic Conference, Washington, D.C., pp. 221-226.

Contents

Introduction 1

Youth Ministry—An Overview 3
    Michael Warren

Part I
Understanding the Task

Faith and the Adolescent 12
    Alfonso M. Nebreda, S.J.

Education for Faith 39
    Alfonso M. Nebreda, S.J.

Evangelization of Youth 47
    Michael Warren

Catholic Education as Evangelization 58
    Jose' M. Calle

Social Processes in Adolescent Catechism 66
    Michael Warren

Part II
Setting Up Programs

Components of Successful Youth Catechetical Programs 84
    Michael Warren

Catholic High Schools: Organizing the
Religion Department 93
    Louis Dalton, C.F.X.

Principles and Procedures in Youth Ministry 115
    Richard Costello and Michael Warren

The ACEC Experiment: A Multiple-Parish
Approach to High School Religious Education 125
    Thomas Zanzig

Understanding the Weekend Format 141
    Michael Warren

Part III
Leadership Development

Christian Experience Weekends: Role of the Director 154
    Michael Warren

Effective Ministry to Youth..162
    Merton P. Strommen

Leadership Training: A Case History 172
    Michael Warren

Adolescent Girls: A Two-Year Study.....................................184
    Gisela Konopka

Resource Guide for Youth Ministry 205
    Michael Warren

Introduction

The idea for this book of readings grew out of a course in youth ministry I taught in the summer of 1975 at three different universities. Students in the course all responded to certain of the assigned readings with much more enthusiasm and appreciation than to others. Some of those readings were from such hard-to-get sources that I had to carry them around with me all summer and go through an awkward and expensive xeroxing process in order to make them available in sufficient numbers for the students.

It occurred to me that if these readings could be gathered into a single reader, they would be available and helpful to far more than could ever find out about them through a summer course. I made a list of them which sat tucked away at a corner of my desk for months, until Robert Heyer of Paulist Press encouraged me to consider editing a book of readings in youth ministry. This book is the result, and all the readings so prized by those students of 1975 appear here.

In order to complete the book I have added several of my own pieces on aspects of youth ministry, some of them up to now unpublished. They appear almost by default, since a search for useful writing on youth ministry shows that there is still far too little writing being done on this topic. Although many fascinating and promising projects in youth ministry are underway throughout the country, those familiar with or responsible for these projects for some reason have not yet shared their efforts with others through writing.

Now that this book is compiled, I see that my greatest hope for it is to encourage others active in youth ministry to take the time and the considerable trouble needed to write of their efforts and insights. Such writing is a very special "ministry to the ministers," and it is badly needed. If such writing is encouraged by this book, the effort the editor has put into it will have been worthwhile.

Youth Ministry—
An Overview

Michael Warren

Ten years ago the term "youth ministry" was, for Catholics, one that had distinctly Protestant overtones. Catholics did not speak much about ministry or ministries to youth. They spoke rather of teaching religion in Catholic high schools or in CCD (Confraternity of Christian Doctrine) programs or they spoke of CYO (Catholic Youth Organization). The language today has changed. That change reflects a change in the way many think of youth and of the way the Church should serve the needs of youth. Where did these changes come from? How can we account for this shift? What does this shift in emphasis mean? Are we, for instance, abandoning our previous commitments to Catholic high schools, to CCD, and to CYO?

The best way of understanding the contemporary phenomenon of youth ministry in the Catholic Church is by situating it within the context of developments in the wider Church. That context will provide the best vantage point for examining both the characteristics of youth ministry in today's Church and those matters that must be attended to in the near future to ensure the further development of this ministry.

Youth Ministry in the Context of the Church

One could claim that out of Vatican II continues to emerge a broader, more comprehensive vision of the mission of the Church. Based on a theology better unified and integrated than in the days of seminary tracts and treatises, pastoral efforts appear to be moving toward convergence. There is a desire for closer coordination of varied ministries, so that these efforts, seemingly quite different in themselves, can be orchestrated to support each other. Thus a unified theology tends naturally toward a unified pastoral action. Another factor influencing the convergence of ministries has been the new consciousness of women as regards their role in the Church. In recent years many women have moved from their traditional works in hospitals and schools into a wide variety of ministries. These women are bringing to their pastoral efforts a freshness of vision and a sense of how various pastoral efforts should relate with one another. An example of this broad vision among nuns can be found in The Network, a coalition of American nuns reaching out from a tiny office near Capitol Hill in Washington into every diocese of the country, to raise political consciousness and marshal political action. These Sisters see their political efforts as a dimension of the pastoral mission of the Church.

It is not surprising that these factors have led persons active in a variety of ministries to young people to consolidate and unify their efforts, especially over the past few years. Thus, within a recent three-year period almost a third of all Catholic dioceses combined their efforts to minister to youth into either a single office or a single person charged with directing this ministry. In many dioceses there had been three separate agencies serving youth: the youth division of the religious education/catechetical office; the Catholic Youth Organization, which carried on non-school-based (but often highly educational) programs; and the Catholic high schools' organization. Often enough, these agencies, working separately, ended up competing with each other in the struggle for adequate funding and even in the matter of programming. What seems to have allowed them to unify under a common effort is the concept of youth ministry.

Youth Ministry

What then is youth ministry, as it is currently developing in the American Catholic Church? Most briefly, it is a comprehensive effort on the part of the Church to serve a broad range of the needs of youth. It is a determination on the part of the community to be identified by young people as a community of care. It is a program to serve the total person and not just the doctrinal understanding of the adolescent. Another way of phrasing the aim of youth ministry: it is an effort on the part of the beloved community to welcome young people into the midst of a rich and enriching communal existence. Youth ministry is the community's stance of welcome toward young people, a stance characterized by gentleness and friendship. Eventually youth ministry will lead to deep commitments on the part of youth, but these commitments will emerge from the inner life of a community and will not be seen as alienating demands imposed by an impersonal organization.

The need for a broadened ministry to young people leading to incorporation in the beloved community is becoming more and more obvious and acute. Many dioceses now find their Catholic youth affiliating with various Christian fundamentalist groups, whose youth programs provide quick fellowship and ready answers from Scripture. What seems especially appealing to Catholic youth in these groups is an ambiance of friendship and caring. It is clearly time for Catholic ministry to youth to move away from highly abstracted doctrinal instruction and to contexts where groups can rediscover the Catholic tradition as a unified story that can be ritually enacted and retold in the light of one's own life story. In a renewed youth ministry Catholics are in fact being faithful to an older tradition of the Church, in which prayerful communities grow in faith through song and dance and meals and through the struggle to care for each other and make sense out of life.

Youth ministry, then, attends to the four basic ministries of the Church: the ministry of the word, including evangelization and catechesis; the ministry of worship; the ministry of guidance and education; and the ministry of healing. Each one of these ministries needs the support of the others if the Church is to be a credible presence among young people. Far from being in competition with one another, those ministering to the young must consciously affirm and encourage the ministries of their colleagues in related areas. In addition, if the Church is to have credibility among the young, these ministries must be open-handed, that is, extended to all young people, regardless of whether they are members of the Church community or not. To affirm open-handed ministry is of course not to deny a privileged place for the ministry of the word, which is an active summons to join the beloved community itself through conversion to Jesus and His Gospel.

Those engaged in youth ministry are currently struggling to discern guiding principles for their efforts. These principles are not emerging from ivory tower theologizing but rather from active engagement in ministry itself and from reflection on pastoral practice. Among these guiding insights one would have to include the following five.

1. Ministry to youth takes into consideration the total situation of young people, including the broad range of their needs. Within this broad range of needs, ministry to youth does not neglect the religious needs of the young. The task of understanding the situation of young people is accomplished first by entering that situation especially through presence and dialogue, and, secondly, by attention to the research being done among young people.

2. The primal ministry to youth is the ministry of friendship. Since the relational needs of youth are especially acute, special attention must be given to creating healthy relationships between the generations. The kind of friendship fostered should be appropriate to the differences in the ages of the adult and the young person. Thus, this relationship tends to be of the aunt/uncle or mentor type. Youth ministry also takes special care to foster peer friendships among young people.

3. Ministry to youth functions out of an affirmation of gifts; that is, it calls young people to recognize and develop their unique gifts. In order to affirm gifts, youth ministry pays close attention to the specialness of each person and to each person's personal development.

4. Ministry to youth is a call to community. It calls young people to recognize their common unity with others as a way of understanding their common humanity. Within the context of this call to community, young people are called also to the com-

munity united by awareness of the presence of the Lord Jesus.

5. Ministry to youth eventually calls youth themselves to ministry. Such a call is in keeping with the nature of ministry, which is to call those being ministered to, to recognize and accept their own ministry. Thus youth ministry is not just a call to participation in programs but rather to active involvement in ministry itself. Ministry *to* youth if it is to be effective must become a ministry *of* youth.

Once young people served by the community accept their own legitimate ministry, a youth ministry program turns an important corner. Its dynamism now comes from within the group, because that group now has become Church and is characterized by the ecclesial community's sense of being both called and sent. At this point the task of those directing youth ministry becomes one of helping the young develop skills needed for effective ministry.

The Future of Youth Ministry

An excellent illustration of the kind of tasks facing youth ministry in the future could be found in the first national conference on ministry to young adults, which met in Washington, D.C. in 1976. Sponsored by the United States Catholic Conference, the meeting was especially noteworthy because of the people who attended it. Almost a third of the participants were young adults under twenty-five years of age, all of whom were either working full-time in ministry or seeking to move from part-time into full-time service. While some saw their full-time ministry as a limited-time commitment in their present lives, most expressed a desire to make a career of lay ministry in the Church.

Most of these young ministers came to ministry through being members of youth retreat teams or through taking part in campus ministry programs that eventually summoned them to their own ministry. They reported receiving the supervision and support they needed to grow in their work. However, almost all who hoped to make ministry a career expressed fears about fu-

ture job stability and financial security. One young man put the
matter this way: "I don't expect ever to become well-off or even
financially comfortable from my ministry, but I know I must be
able to support a family if I am to stay in ministry. What I want
to know is, are there people and places in the Church willing to
take me and my ministry seriously enough to provide me a fair
salary?"

The answer to this young minister's question cannot be
given at the present time. It will have to evolve over time. However, at all levels of the Church, those concerned about ministry
to youth will have to attend to such pragmatic issues. Young
people looking for a career in ministry need advocates who will
be sensitive to the financial and job security aspects of their
ministry. Put more simply, those of us who were instrumental in
calling these young people to ministry must continue to attend to
their legitimate needs and alert others to those needs.

Another matter that must be attended to for the future of
youth ministry is that of more active collaboration and sharing
by leaders in similar aspects of work with youth. Directors of
youth retreat programs, heads of Catholic high school religion
departments, leaders in youth liturgy and other programs of
worship are some of the persons whose sharing could be most
fruitful for a rapidly evolving ministry. More collaboration is
also needed for special areas that need more attention. One such
area is that of education for mature sexuality. It is indefensible
that such an important need of young people has gotten so little
systematic attention in the American Church.

A third area for future attention is the matter of ministry to
young adults. This ministry looms on the horizon as one of
special importance. The large numbers of young adults in the
United States and the relative neglect of their needs by the
churches is finally being recognized and faced. However, active
ministry to young adults has hardly begun and has not yet
touched many of their keenest needs, such as the need for intelligent marriage preparation, for group and individual counsel,
and for a catechesis suited to their special age and mentality.

The above overview of contemporary youth ministry may
help the reader understand why some see the area of youth min-

istry as one of the most exciting areas in today's Church. Youth ministry is discovering its own way as it goes, traveling often enough along routes up to now untried and uncharted. In its own small way, youth ministry seems to be an important part of an exciting renewal of ministry in the entire Church. Having a part in a wider effort affecting the entire Church should give much joy to those ministering to young people.

Part I

Understanding the Task

Faith and
the Adolescent

Alfonso M. Nebreda, S.J.

Alfonso Nebreda is one of the leading catechetical thinkers in
the Catholic Church. Since the 1950's his writings have had a
key influence on the Church's understanding of its pastoral mission. As a young Jesuit missionary in Japan after World War II,
he discovered that it was easier to introduce to the Gospel a Japanese who had only a vague idea of the tenets of Christianity
than it was to deal with a baptized European for whom the Gospel was "old hat" and eminently dismissable.

The following two-part article by Father Nebreda was originally
an oral presentation given to catechists in Australia and later
transcribed from a tape recording. The oral character of Nebreda's presentation gives it a stimulating freshness and immediacy.
Nebreda focuses again and again on seminal issues related to the
development of faith. The reader will note underlying his ideas
an entire philosophy of the ministry of the word, that is, of the
process of leading both individuals and communities to maturity
of faith.

Some of the important questions he addresses are: How does adolescent faith growth fit into the context of a lifetime of growth
in faith? How should a minister to youth understand the freedom
necessary for a true act of faith? What is the relationship between the catechist's own faith and the faith one is trying to nurture in young people? What is the role of the environment within
which one proposes Christian faith?

Nebreda's ideas will be valuable for all involved in ministry to youth, particularly to religion teachers, catechists, and parents. He presents these persons with a framework for great patience and much hope in dealing with the young.   *Michael Warren*

────────────── ▲ ──────────────

Part I

My subject is: "Faith and the Adolescent". I will here concentrate on the first word—Faith; because you know more about the adolescent than I could ever attempt to know. So I will try to zero in for a while here (and again in later articles) on some basic assumptions that I think need correction, or challenge when we talk so openly and readily about faith. Instead of giving you theories, I might as well introduce the topic with something that happened here in Sydney two years ago but could have happened now in any part of the world. A Jesuit was asking me, obviously in pain and suffering, "What do you say to parents and teachers who come and say, 'what happened to my boy or to my girl that they don't believe anymore? These teenagers!' " Well it is quite a tall order to answer that but I will try to approach it from different angles, as much as I can. Because in that question itself there are already assumptions that need challenging, that need clarification.

Parental Concern

The first thing that this question brought to my mind was something that happened to me in Spain, of all places, 13 years ago. I was giving my first seminar in my own country on catechetics, in Comillas, northern Spain with 150 men coming from high school (from your college level). Since many of these people had been my colleagues before and some of them my own teachers, I was very cagey about coming straight to the problem. But the second day, things started moving. I remember they were asking me similar questions: "How can you explain that so many of our kids whom you know, after being with us for as long as 10 years, go to the University and then *lose* their faith?" The first day I would have hesitated to do this, but the second day, I felt I could take the risk. I chuckled and said, "Who told you that they had faith to begin with?" That was the assumption those parents were making. How come the children lost faith? You cannot lose something you did not have. So I said, "Are you sure they had faith?" "What do you mean by that?" "That's exactly what I want you to discuss. What do you mean by faith?"

Likewise, I remember meeting a former graduate of a very well known Jesuit School in Spain one day. I had known through his parents that he didn't go to church anymore. So I met the boy, a very wholesome simple boy and I said, "What's wrong with you, Bob? They tell me you don't go to church." And he was just as serious. "But Father, be sensible, being a boarder with you people for eight or ten years, I think I have had enough masses to last me my whole life. Don't you think so? I think I can take a good holiday for a couple of years and nothing will be wrong!" Now, what would you answer to that? Since I was talking to Jesuits at that time, I told them, "You chew that among yourselves."

Automatic Belief?

This gently or not so gently obliging your teenagers to go to mass everyday, see what it leads to? As soon as they leave your school they ask this silly question which shows clearly that all those masses were for the birds . . . they were a facade concealing an emptiness which we didn't do anything to fill in the most important and formative years perhaps in which the Church as an institution had them within her fold. We are afraid of taking risks as a lot of parents are. And we didn't allow them to grow in the process. Now, why did we do that? Because we thought that since they had been baptized—and their baptism was obviously valid—they had been in very good Catholic homes, they belonged to a good Catholic parish and they were in excellent Catholic schools or Catholic milieu, automatically, naturally they were going to be believers. Nonsense! Nobody is automatically a believer. Let me analyze this for a while.

I am not going to give you little ready-made gimmicks. You don't need them anyhow even if I had them. What I want is to go in depth to realize that we are dealing here with the most mysterious and wonderful of all realities that demands from all of us a change of heart. In our work we take too much for granted, we demand too much, we expect too much—and we don't *hope* enough. Does this sound like a riddle? Let me explain.

We expect too much and by expectation, in our technological society, it means that we push a button and normally, unless the machine is broken, it's going to give us a Coca-cola or a Lemonade or I don't know what. Otherwise, we blame the machine. You see, you expect to get that. Or you put your money in this bank and you expect to get some profit, and so on. Well, forget that type of expectation. You are not dealing with a thing like that. We have too many expectations which normally are illusions and they are the mother of all the 'disillusions' we suffer in our lives. If we didn't have illusions, we wouldn't have 'disillusions'. As simple as that. But we don't have enough hope, which means that we know and believe that God is alive and God cares for these kids infinitely more than all of us will ever care. They are in good hands. We are servants with a specific and important job to do but a very very humble ministry; servants, I repeat, that's what we are.

Baptism and Belief

Now, the first assumption therefore that we have to dismantle is the idea that because our children were baptized, they already believed. Baptism does not give faith that way. What does baptism do for our children? It does give them what we technically call the "habit of faith" which is the power, the inclination, the attraction to make an act of faith. But naturally, it doesn't give the *act* of faith which is something they have to act out. The fact that we baptized them (and I have very good reasons to still insist on the importance of infant baptism) does not in the least imply that automatically things are going to be fine.

The first Church as a rule baptized only those who had been evangelized and converted; it was dealing mainly with adults. Our churches today—for the other Christian churches have similar problems—do not know what to do with those who have been baptized but for all purposes are not converted or evangelized. How to convert those who have been baptized? You will realize this better if you keep in mind, as I am going to explain presently, that in order to understand the dynamics of faith, the model is not a child who is not a person yet but at best a promise of a person, a seed of a person that has to develop. In a sense we could say that we begin building the house of faith from the roof. In the case of an adult, baptism is supposed to crown the whole process of Faith.

Wrong Start?

Now with our children we begin these where the adult convert ends. So, unless we bring our adolescents by degrees to the level where that community act that was their baptism means something in their lives through conversion and personal faith, we cannot speak except about "baptized-not-yet believers." We have them by the million in our churches even if they happen to go to mass every Sunday. But we have them naturally by hundreds in our schools and in our CCD program. We should not be astonished about that, especially in a growing pluralistic society in which most of the values by which our society lives contradict the very values that the Gospel is proclaiming. We shouldn't be astonished about that.

When I baptize a baby, I make a point, no matter what the congregation is, to say a few words. And I say, "What is going to happen to this baby? Is it going to be a saint? A great man or a great woman? Is it going to be a rascal, a criminal? Who knows? Let us pray, because the only thing we can do is very simple but very important. We can *pray* that they become great. We can *hope*—and we will never hope enough—and we can and contagiously must *be*, that contagiously we may lead them; because that is as much as we can do with a free being: by the attraction of a contagious goodness around him, show him how beautiful it is to be good. More than that we cannot do."

Becoming: A Task

I was born a man but I have to become human. And this *becoming* is the most beautiful and the most ambiguous of all processes. This is not something that happens automatically, biologically, matter of fact, so to say. Every other organism (the sphere of my body included) has a one track growth. You see a little dog and it grows to a certain extent and that's it. Provided the environment gives him what he needs to grow. Any plant or any animal, our own body included, *becomes* in a kind of one dimensional process of progress.

But this simply does not hold true of the personal level. There are a lot of books that even speak about "On Becoming a Person." Even linguistically, we are misleading people when we speak about "becoming a person" as if that would be something that happens by itself—as our body grows, whether you think of it or not. You do not *become* a person that way. You have to make yourself a person by a painful, active, demanding process of action and reaction, of responsibility, of freedom. And that is essentially an ambiguous, ambivalent movement which easily leads to regression—not only progression.

No wonder psychologists, when they discuss the mystery of a person, use always descriptive names that give the same idea. "A person is a task,"—a task which is never fully fulfilled. "A person is a job." "A person is a mission"—never accomplished. "A person is a growth." "A person is a movement." "A person is a project,"—a project for life. "A person is a process." Now, all these descriptions are bound to give us a clue but we forget it constantly because we don't realize that faith takes hold of the person; not of my brain, not of my stomach or of my blood pressure, but of my *person*. That is why it is very ambiguous and highly questionable to speak about *having faith*. It is the other way around. Faith *has* me, if I let it do so; it takes hold of my personality and shapes it into a new creature, a new way of being myself. Now, the root of that process, freedom, remains untouchable. That very freedom which is the necessary condition for love. That is why God made us free so that we may be able to love. But in the moment we are free, literally we can say "no" to God. And if I can say "no" to God, should you be astonished that I can say "no" to you?

Freedom and Response

A lot of parents and educators seem to forget this. Our kids do have the terrible power to say "no" to God. Should we be astonished? That we are pained, it is understandable. But we shouldn't be astonished that from time to time suddenly they say, "No, Sister," "No, Father," "No, Brother." We have to overcome the tendency (that is still too alive in many circles) to see faith in static, negative terms. Static—like a jewel, like a treasure, like a deposit? Or negative: as long as I don't throw away my faith, the faith I got in baptism, faith stays with me. No, it's the opposite: as long and only as long as I exercise that faith which is a constant "yes" to God, Faith has me.

Faith Is Dynamic

Sometimes, even among priests and religious, when somebody suddenly just throws away everything, people tend to think, "What happened to him yesterday, now?" It is a long, long process of a living organism just simply ceasing to operate. What happens to your hand if you don't move it for a few weeks, months? Something goes wrong. You cannot move it again normally. The same is true of faith. We tend to look at the outcome instead of considering the whole *process* in which this active faith, this power to say "yes" to God, has not been exercised.

None other than the present Prefect of the Sacred Congregation for Religious Education, Cardinal Garrone, when he was still Bishop in France, wrote about 15 or 16 years ago, something that may shock you. He said, "If your adolescents don't resent religion, beware, something is terribly wrong." The majority of us, parents and teachers, expect the opposite. We think that the opposite is the norm. Now, your son from being such a nice eight years old altar boy who was also happy with all the things that he got in school, in CCD and so on, now at 15 or 16, is he going to keep and show exactly the same attitude? Well, you should know better. Everything in his person has changed or is in the process of changing—radically. And you mean to tell me that the most all-pervasive, demanding and deep-seated reality which commands the whole of him—faith, is going to remain unruffled and untouched? Especially in a pluralistic society like ours? It is much more realistic to conclude that either the boy is stupid or he couldn't care less. Take your pick. Either way, faith is not respected.

Project: Becoming Christian

So, if becoming a person is such a demanding and difficult thing, becoming a Christian—which follows the same dynamics, is a very delicate, patient job to be performed. Already in the second century that great layman, Tertullian could say that "Christians are not born, they have to become." I cannot believe once and for all, any more than I can *be*, exist once and for all. Believing is the unfolding of my life of Faith as existing is the unfolding of my existence.

Well, these are basic elements that don't touch specific concrete responses. But unless we think of the problem of faith in those terms, we may be satisfied with something that should make us jittery, and we may be nervous when in fact we should calmly meet the obvious development of growth in our children.

Love Is Not a Conscript

But there is something else that I want to say before we conclude,—something I have already insinuated. Do you realize that even God cannot make me love if I don't want to? We can command the body of our children. We can physically make them go with us to mass. Can you command his heart or her heart? Can you change it? And this is what is required in order to believe. A *change of heart*. That is the best definition of conversion. As Vatican II in No. 5 of the Constitution on Divine Revelation reminds us, conversion is a changing of the heart and turning of it to *God*.

Is there here anybody who knows how to reach the heart of a child? Of an adolescent? Is there anybody who can make people love? I would like to meet this person, because God Himself seems to find the task difficult. Remember Augustine's saying, "God who created you without you will not save you without you." Many of us, whether administrators or teachers or parents, talk glibly about converting people, about making them be; about convincing them. You can convince them all right but you cannot convert them. There is a tremendous gap between convincing somebody and converting him. Conversion is clearly the job of God,—the Almighty God who can mysteriously work out this miracle of changing the heart without doing violence to it.

We will talk about that in more detail later, but I want you to ponder on this because, as I say, we all approach the tremendous, the awesome task that the Lord has entrusted to us with such a naive expectation that naturally leads to an impasse. It is a miracle in our job if we can maintain a certain amount of optimism ourselves. It will only be possible if we have a clear idea of what the Lord expects from us, which is something very definite,—important but modest.

Faith and Certitude

Before I close, just let me leave with you this very simple thought. We talk so easily about faith as if we knew for sure who has Faith and who hasn't Faith. That shows again the dreadful consequences of this conventional Christianity into which we were born. To be concrete, if you ask me, "Father Nebreda, are you sure you have faith?", what do you think I could answer? Theologically, the only valid answer would be for me to say, "I hope so." I hope so. Do you realize this? When that father was saying, "My goodness, what went wrong with my children? They don't believe anymore?" that, of course implied that they once believed. Why? Because they have identified believing, faith— which is a new creation—with certain ways of doing things, with a certain mentality, with certain actions. Well, that is a very poor and very shallow way of approaching things. I repeat, Anyone of us, the best we can say to somebody who asks us, "Do you believe?", is to say, truly and not as a gimmick, "I hope so." Because if I were sure that I believe—as many of us are—then this would be tantamount to being sure that I am saved. And the Council of Trent was very wise in reminding us that nobody, as long as he is on earth, is sure of being saved. Living faith, and this is what we are talking about today, is eternal life. Already, now! So, the only thing we can do about this is to hope—because this is a tremendous grace. We are confident, we hope; we are not sure like that.

What would you feel if I say to you that, aside from our Lord, of course and our Lady, strictly speaking, there are very very few Christians on earth. We have all kinds of pagans, ourselves included, in different stages of conversion. That is what we have.

Mellowed Approach

Then you will see that our approach to the problem of the faith of our adolescents would be much more sensible, much more mellow, much more human and divine if we would admit from the beginning that we are fellow travelers in a very risky journey in which all what we have is our unshakable hope in God's mercy and in God's love. Because there is nothing that makes our youngsters more suspicious and resentful—and with reason—than this crystal-clear total assurance that we teachers and elders seem to show them in answering questions, etc., as if everything would be clear. If everything is clear nothing is clear.

It means that we have reduced God to a very tiny little idol that we can control. But God is not an idol. God simply refuses to be encompassed by such a petty way of thinking. Instead of getting jittery, getting nervous, getting frustrated, we should turn around the whole approach and realize that our adolescents are the best help that God is putting in our way to lead us to a more humble awareness of His greatness and His grace. A real stimulus to become everyday a little more *faithful* ourselves. Faith-full!

The idea of faith should constantly, I say, be kept where it belongs—within the parameter of the personality growth. Every adolescent of every era but particularly our youth today are in a moment where they need more than a lot of people telling them from the outside what it's like to be a believer: they need someone to show them from within how beautiful it is to grow painfully, humbly into a man or a woman of faith.

Vanishing Adolescent

A few years ago in the States, a famous psychologist wrote a delightful and thought-provoking book under the title "The Vanishing Adolescent." His thesis, which I think is very valid throughout the world in our technological society, is that the problem with our adolescents is simply a projection of the real problem of our society, which is that we have very few real adults. And without adults the adolescent does not know how to become himself. He is lost in the search for identity. He may resent the adults but he needs them in order to know his place and to gropingly find his future. If that is true psychologically, I would say that this is infinitely more true theologically.

The problem in our Church, we could say, is not the vanishing Catholic adolescent! The problem is that there are very few Catholic adults. There are very few people who have reached that level in which they deal with God as an adult deals with a person. You know how an adult, the truly adult, deals with persons: accepting them as they are, not as they should be or I want them to be for me, to take them as they are. The Gospel injunction, "unless you turn around and become like a child you don't qualify for the Kingdom of heaven," shows more clearly that this is far cry from asking us to become childish. It is a stimulus to be childlike which is possible only for a real adult.

The Key Question

Therefore, in order to stir up your own reflection, I wish to ask you candidly: How is your own spiritual situation in regard to your own faith? Because if that is in good health, I don't foresee any big problem about your task. You will be frustrated, of course. You ask any mother who has adolescent children and she can tell you. We will have many problems, many painful and exasperating moments of depression but basically, things will be all right. The Lord will be able to use you even when you think that you are being absolutely hopeless in your effort to reach the heart of your children. Because I don't care what you feel one day or one week or for a few months or even years. One day you may be astonished to see what God did through you when you had no idea that the seed you had planted and you thought wasted, ten years or fifteen years later comes to surprise you and blossoms into something that is going to grow and thrive. But the basic point is that only life gives life. Only life gives life—and faith is "essentially life."

It is not a question of talking about life. What is life? If we are alive, people will sense it and with some kind of powerful contagion touch and transform them. Even when our own verbiage, all our conceptual barrage seems to be an obstruction to the transmission, in mysterious ways our living witness will carry through and be prolonged in their lives.

PART II

Life and Love

I am going to try to simply zero in on a definition that is pretty well-known to you and yet, it is very thought-provoking, I think, for the topic at hand: the definition which sees faith as the interpersonal communion of life and love with God. It is an interpersonal communion of life and love between God and the adolescent in Christ. That offers us, I think, a couple of pointers to just try to put together a few thoughts, first, about the idea of life and second, around the idea of love.

Life is one thing and it is another thing to talk about life. I remember the time I had to instruct a Japanese lady who was married to a Filipino gentleman. She really wanted to become a Catholic for very good reasons. But, she didn't have anybody who spoke Japanese and she had got all kinds of Catholic books including a Japanese Catechism. Instead of helping this literature complicated her life no end. She said, "My goodness, Father, if I am going to make sense of all that this book says I don't think I am intelligent enough to understand it even if I spent my whole life on it." So, I had to respond to her in the way I now often respond to others. I said: Life is one thing. All of us who are alive have a good idea of what life is. But if we are asked to define life, not only ourselves but even the most exceptionally gifted doctor or biologist could spend a whole lifetime trying to define life, trying to explain life, and would probably never succeed. We tend to forget this. I chuckle when I hear people say that we have to be accurate and adequate in presenting religion. Even the greatest theological genius is just desperately trying to explain the impossible. Only God knows God and we have forgotten that pretty much. There has been a constant tradition in the Church (which is still particularly alive in the East) of the so-called negative theology that we need to be reminded of. Even the greatest theologian is saying all kinds of nonsense about God because *only God knows God*.

Doctrine and Life

But if we are alive, as I say, we know somehow what life is. Yet, can you teach life?

I think that we can get a kind of valuable insight here from a little conversation that the late Japanese Premier Ikeda had with Pope John XXIII. Prime Minister Ikeda was the real architect of the Japanese economic miracle because he was Minister of Finance for the crucial years before becoming Premier himself. When he met the Pope about twelve or thirteen years ago, although he was a Buddhist, Ikeda was so impressed by this old man that returning to Japan he openly referred to his visit to the Pope in his next Speech to the Nation. Then he went on to say to his countrymen: "Begin now to get worried. People the world over speak of the Japanese Miracle. What miracle is that? We have still to find something much more difficult yet far more important, namely, how do you make man? How do you build people because that is what we need in Japan."

I would say that he was voicing a concern that applies to all of us. Again: Can you teach Life? The whole field of education seems to be now in utter disarray. If by education you mean passing over certain tools, certain knowledge of a culture to the next generation, that indeed is something possible. But is that education? What I mean to say is, if we understand what education is with all its tremendous challenges and limitations, we begin to be a lot more modest and begin to be aware of the problem of religious education. Because here we are dealing with the most delicate and highest type of life you can think of.

Attitudes

Father Calle in his little book, "Catechesis for the 70's," appropriately says that "religious ignorance" is not so much the absence of religious knowledge as the lack of religious attitudes. Indeed, "religious ignorance," so often decried nowadays as one of the roots of the evils in the Church, is a very misleading expression. Unless you make a distinction. If by religious ignorance is meant not knowing additional bits of religious information, the answer is: Is that so terribly important? But if what is involved is the absence of religious attitudes, then you had better watch out.

Now, there are no attitudes without some kind of cognitive content, even if this remains inarticulated, and unreflected upon.

But the reverse is not necessarily true, as we know by painful experience. To think that knowledge of itself leads to or brings about a corresponding change in attitude is to forget that attitude is, as the Japanese beautifully expressed it in their language, "the posture of the heart." Attitude is the total personality in action. Now, the great American psychologist Gordon Allport could well say that attitudes are "not taught but caught." If our children didn't have any point of reference in their experience and their environment as far as life is concerned, you couldn't do a thing. You would be talking to them in a foreign language. That is why, hopefully, in the school, in the home and in yourself they can see, before you can say a word, that there is something vital and real in what you try to convey. This is again the sense of contagiousness, the ambiental witness we spoke about, with all the importance that we tend to minimize, especially when we think of the community which a home is and the community which a school should be, and a community which a parish should be but most of the time isn't.

Climate and Growth

Since we are dealing with life, it is as simple as this. If you have a very very healthy baby and you put him in a T.B.-ridden atmosphere, before you know it the baby is a T.B. patient. And if you have a very weak and sickly child, the first thing you do is to try to look for a healthy environment in which you may appeal to the sources, the hidden forces of this organism to little by little grow to health.

What would you say of an environment which, as far as faith is concerned, is for all purposes a morgue? No matter how beautiful your explanations in religious education are, when children go back and they enter into that morgue-like atmosphere, all you have said makes no sense; it frustrates, perhaps. As I said, there are no techniques to produce life. Life is only begotten by life. This expression of St. Paul should always be uppermost in our minds when we reflect on or discuss teaching, talking about faith.

Faith and Life

Faith comes from life because it is life. It has to be like a contagion. Both Harnack and Loisy, writing on the first centuries, could say that Christianity spread like a wild fire by a phenomenal contagion of hope. Phenomenal contagion of hope, meaning that faith appears truly to those people as something to feel hopeful about. They understood well the challenge of the writer of the First Epistle of Peter, 3:15 urging every Christian of this time, "Be always ready with your defense whenever you are called to account for the hope that is in you." That hope, of course, is faith. If the hope is there, one way or another it will become contagious because there is nothing that people need more and want more than hope. Now, when you look around and see many of our teachers, very good persons, but with so little hope shining through them, whose message seems to be: "It is so difficult to be a Christian," should you be astonished to hear that people don't want to come to CCD classes or anything else? That is not a thing you can make up for. If there is no hope in us, we are literally hopeless, hopeless, hopeless. Without any adjective added to that indictment: hopeless! Now, what can a hopeless instrument, what can a hopeless proclaimer of Good News achieve?

What To Do?

What can we do in this regard? The best we can do is to try to introduce God to this child and this child to God. But this introduction even by common sense in any society demands at least two things: *that we know God and that we know the child.* Except in a very formalistic and hollow situation, the least people normally expect is that when somebody introduces two persons, he should know them both to a certain extent. "This is Mr. Brown, this is Mrs. White." You know both. But to know both in Biblical and personalist language is equivalent to being acquainted with, to being familiar with, to being friendly with. In plain language, biblically as well as personally, "to know" is a synonym for "to love." Believe it or not, for the Bible—and, if you understood it correctly for a true personalistic approach as well—it is not true to say that you have first to know someone and then hopefully you will love him. If this is true when dealing with human beings, it is much more so in dealing with God: you have to love Him in order to know Him.

Prejudice

Newman, in a very powerful passage in one of his sermons, appropriately says, nobody will come to know God unless he is or becomes prejudiced for God. Nobody will come to know God unless he is (this is a Christian) or becomes (this is a convert) prejudiced in favor of God. In the whole theology and psychology of Faith for Newman, the idea of prejudice is very prominent. Indeed, Newman is a hundred years ahead of his time as far as the theology of faith is concerned—as in many other things. When he speaks about prejudice he is referring to something that we should do well to explore further. By the way, Gordon Allport in his book *The Nature of Prejudice* offers also many insights along the same lines. Prejudice is not, (as we tend to think according to the present usage in most European languages, English included) something necessarily negative. We hear for example "He is prejudiced against the Negroes" or "He has prejudices against Asians" etc. Of itself prejudice can be either positive or negative. You can be prejudiced against; you can be prejudiced in favor.

Now, this idea of prejudice is so important because it reflects the wholistic (as anthropologists call it) character of the person and therefore of faith. We often say: someone has prejudices. Strictly speaking, we don't *have* prejudices. We *are* prejudiced. Why? Because the strength of a prejudice is the same as the strength of my personality. Prejudice, as any European language already suggests, is a previous judgment. If somebody knew me well enough he could, so to say, forecast how I was going to react to a person, to an event, to a book, to a show, etc. He could say: "Father Nebreda will love that music," or "he would not like that film."—if he knew me well enough.

Why? Because I am myself. Now, who am I? The result of a thousand influences; all that I have seen, heard, experienced, my whole life is truly the weight of my prejudice. There, at the root of my heart, is where I have to find the source of either my orientation towards God or my orientation away from God. Newman is very subtle. He is simply putting in contemporary language what the Bible says. You have to come to love God, to be in favor of God in order to actually know Him. Don't you remember the third chapter of St. John when the Lord says, "those who love the light come to the light, those who hate the light avoid it lest their works may be shown for what they are"? But, as you well know, for John the light is a name for Jesus: "I am the light of the world." So, the Lord is simply saying, "Those who love me come to me. They know me. Those who don't like me they don't come." Read the whole first Epistle of John and you'll find there repeated time and again the same thing.

More on Introductions

"To know," then, is the same as "to love" in personal terms and in religious terms. Therefore, when I said very simply: if you want some kind of clue on what to do with your children, with your adolescents, you are called to introduce God to them and them to God; but that presupposes that you know both some-how—I was just implying thereby something infinitely more demanding; something we have to fight for all our lives long: to love God and to love them!

The first point introduces us to the whole realm of our spiritual life. How close are we to God? What is our experience of God? We could prolong this examination of conscience for a long, long time; but I would rather like to insist a little more on the second point. Do we really know our children? Do we really know them? The answer to that question must be predicated on a second question: do we love them as they are?

Loving and Needing

Many of us—priests, religious, because of our vocation, tend to become a functional type of animal which needs people because otherwise we wouldn't have a job. *Needs people.* I need people otherwise if I didn't have an audience like you, what would I be doing right now. But if all I do is to give them some of my time and talents because I have made a promise and I am going to teach in the CCD or I have signed a contract and I am going to be in charge of religious education in that school and so on, then that easily ends up by becoming my function. It won't be of much help to anyone, myself included, unless I can transcend such an attitude and realize that these are unique people with needs of their own,—people dearly loved by our common Father who is in Heaven. Therefore it won't do any good just to be able to tolerate them; I'll have to learn how to love them truly.

Prepositional Priority

That is not an easy thing, as you know. With adolescents, even the most wonderful parent at times can get exasperated and not know what to do. But when you have no children of your own to deal with, but 40 different children from different families, after a while if you manage to keep your cool that is indeed a miracle! And, in fact a miracle it must be if it is going to enable us to perform our task properly. But unfortunately the only thing that seems to affect us is that there are things in them we couldn't possibly agree with. Which is only natural if only by the force of the generation gap. But what should actually strike us is that these adolescents are unique people entrusted to us by our Father. Then we probably would be able to do something because together all what we are doing is supposed to be a kind of communication. We are supposed to communicate somehow a message. Well, communication of whatever (in this particular case, communication of Christianity, of the Good News) completely depends on communication *between*. But a communication between requires some communion.

Communication and Communion

Now, what is my communion with this child? If there is no communion whatsoever (communion is another name for love) we will not communicate anything because we are not communicating with them. We have very little in common, except to be branded time and again, as it happens unfortunately, the *enemy*.

Schedule and Persons

So people will say, "Yes, Yes, but I have a program to cover," instead of asking themselves, "do I know my class to begin with?" "I have something to finish." Wait a minute—you have to deal with people. If you don't make sure that you *are* in communion with them, communicating with them, it is useless. If you need one hour, use one hour. If you need 20 hours, use 20 hours till you know that you are somehow communicating, that there is a communication between both of you. Then in a very short time you will be able to get across to them what otherwise you would never have managed to convey.

Programming People?

We have adopted this idea because of our functionalistic approach to our task as religious educators. The Principal will perhaps urge you to cover the whole syllabus because "that is what is the syllabus that we have agreed on." As a result you strongly feel: "I have to finish all this within the next 20 hours, you know." This is theory. In practice you are just talking to them in Greek and as far as I know the kids around you don't understand Greek! Can you honestly be satisfied with such a meaningless performance of a rule when you are not making the slightest impact on your students? Communication is not something that is one way only. It essentially depends on whether the other door is open. If it is closed, you are not communicating. You are just bothering, barking at the door. Making noises and becoming a nuisance. Is that a good way of communicating Good News? No wonder they can and do say: "You know, you are really bad news to me!" This sounds very obvious but unfortunately it is the obvious that we forget. I am reminded here of the famous controversy between the great Protestant theologians Karl Barth and Paul Tillich. Karl Barth was a typically kerygmatic spokesman: "only God, the Divine Majesty." In presenting God he spoke such a language that Paul Tillich couldn't but reply: "Listening to you writing those things I feel as if you wanted to throw the Gospel to people as if you throw a stone." Some of us do that. We are stoning people with the Gospel! Is that a Gospel? If after listening to us people feel, "What a bother, what a nuisance," is that Good News? Paul Tillich went on to add: You should present them the Gospel as if you showed them a piece of good bread when they are hungry. These are indeed well known things, but things which unfortunately we tend to forget.

Examination in Love

So much then, for the idea of life. But I have already in the process entered the second theme which I announced, namely, the point of love. St. Teresa of Lisieux wrote: "In the twilight of our life we will be examined of one thing, *love*." That is the only thing they are going to ask of all of us. I don't care how your *syllabi* look, complete or inadequate, exciting or unexciting. I can only tell you that the final examination, the only one that counts, is going to be a very simple, pointed question: "What did you do? What type of person have you been?" That sounds very general, doesn't it? Well, listen to the Judge: "Did you give something to drink to this person when he or she was thirsty? Somebody was hungry—did you feed him? Somebody was lonely—did you console him?" As simple as that. When you compare the 25th chapter of Matthew, in which the final test on genuine Christianity is beautifully summarized, you wonder whether we are taking the Gospel seriously.

I said, "Faith is a communion of life and love between God and man." I cannot but repeat these truisms because they remain unshakable. What is important is not what we think (concept, concept, concept) and what we say (words, words, words; beautiful or not so beautiful; nice or not so nice; correct or incorrect). That's not at all what counts, but what I *am* and what I *do*. Or, if you want to connect both because ideally both should be connected, what they are going to ask me on the last judgment and I should therefore keep in mind as essential is, what am I doing with what I know? What type of person am I being with what I know?

You see, for us Catholics today, it is good to realize that we are now barely turning a tide that has almost four centuries of bad influence. Catholic theologians four centuries ago (and even more so catechists and religious educators) insisted on the objective side of faith. They accented the intellectual, cognitive elements in faith so strongly that people got the impression that this and only this is *the* important thing. Those theologians' insistence on these elements was an understandable reaction to the Protestant Reformers' one-sided, subjectivistic aspect of faith.

Well, if you are of that conviction—that faith is mainly intellectual—I have very bad news for you. For in a formal analysis, faith does not save because of its cognitive component but because of its attitudinal and behavioral aspects. I repeat. What saves in faith is not what I think (no matter how correct, how orthodox) but what I *do* with what I know. So, if we want those three elements connected, as they should be, we must not naively surmise that mere intellectual emphasis is going to solve the problem. Vatican II has repeatedly decried the scandalous gap in Christians between "knowing" and actual living. Indeed, the total picture of faith implies first, to admit certain truths. Second, and most difficult and important, it means submitting without condition, surrendering without bargain to God in Christ—that is conversion. And third, committing oneself in life, to that very thing I have admitted and to that very Person to whom I have submitted.

Adherence in Faith

Well, again yes, faith is an assent; although instead of this word "assent," (that too often gives the impression of nodding intellectually from outside to something) I prefer the more traditional one of "adherence" which St. Augustine beautifully explored by quoting that famous passage of the psalm: For me it is good to adhere to God, to stick to God. It is the personal attachment whereby I just trust God fully. So I would say *assent* is good, but all depends where I can *consent*. Consent is another name for sympathy. *"Consentire"* means "sympathize with." And faith is nothing short of that. Faith is the result of a newly lighted sympathy between God and man.

St. Thomas in his time could speak about a new knowledge by "connaturality." "You have to become attuned to God in order to understand." It is very interesting to note that many European languages would say that to know a person is only possible if you are "born together." For instance, in French, we have Con-naitre. Paul Claudel has beautiful considerations on this. And these are just insights in modern attire, throwing into new relief what the Bible was very familiar with, but unfortunately, we had forgotten and proceeded more or less to think that you can agree on some notions and therefore you are a believer; you can acquire some ideas and that automatically means Faith!

Knowing and Faith

Do you know who knows most in that sense about God without actually knowing him? The devil. The devil is, so to say, the most accomplished of all pseudo-theologians who know all the ins and outs *about* God. But in the strict theological language, he does not *know* God. Because it is one thing "to know about God;" quite another thing is "to know God." "To know about" means that you reduce God to a thing. You do not need to count on Him to know Him. For instance, that is the way to know about Mathematics or Biology or about anything which is objectified. You have your files. You don't need to consult with this cat in order to take pictures of this cat and so on. You know about this. But when you try to know a person as he or she is, then you have to enter fully into a relationship whereby this person freely consents to open his heart to you. The whole situation is completely changed: from active and conquering (*you* are the one who calls the shots when you are dealing with "knowing about"), you have to become humble and appealing because if you want to know Johnny as he is, you will never know him unless he wants to collaborate. You need him. It all depends this time not on you and your brain, but on whether you can actually convince him to freely open his heart to you and tell you who he is. Then and only then will you be able to know him as he is.

Love in Faith

The same is true of the knowledge which is love in faith. To know God means nothing short of loving Him. That means entering into a new relationship in which I cease to act independently and submit myself to the conditions, adopt the total attitude which may appeal to and open the other of God's self-revelation. Short of that, I will never "know Him."

How often in the Missions we were somehow puzzled by situations we encountered and didn't know how to handle. In the old days when Catholic schools thought they could only justify themselves by holding obligatory, compulsory courses in religious education, Bible, catechesis and so on, every student whether Catholic or not had to attend those courses. Time and again the school would be perplexed and frustrated because the top prizes in Religion would go to somebody who clearly didn't believe and couldn't care less about God. But he or she was very brainy. So you had to give number one to the pagan, an avowed pagan. That should have started them thinking. And the distinction, which is obvious in the Bible, would have struck them at once. This kid knew more than anybody else about God but that doesn't mean he knew God. Nearby you had a boy or a girl, who according to the academic standards, you had a hard time not to flunk because the poor kid did not have much upstairs. He didn't have much of an IQ. And you, in a quandary, puzzled, saying, "My goodness, but we have only 20 Catholics in the whole school of 800 and I am about to flunk one of my Catholic kids, a very good kid at that, and that brainy little fellow there, you know, gets all the prizes!" Well, we should have known better. That poor boy or girl who barely could answer your questions straight may not have known practically much about God. But in his or her way they did know God. They were open and very close to God. See the difference?

The first thing is knowledge in a depersonalized and depersonalizing way: you deal with God as you would deal with any other object. In the other one it means a type of knowledge that is essentially dependent on an interpersonal relation. It is utterly demanding a change of heart, a change of attitude.

Growth towards Selflessness

I don't want to tax your attention but if you ask me for a simple criterion to know whether we are doing a good job, I will always bring you back to essentials. Ask yourselves: are these kids becoming less selfish little by little? If so, wonderful. If not, I couldn't care less about all your educational improvements. You are not doing anything to bring them closer to God. Because coming closer to God means coming closer to opening their hearts. You have to see this by the fruits. And these fruits have to be seen not only by you but by those at home. They—the family—will tell you, the gang will tell you whether these adolescents are becoming more themselves by being open to the others or not. Otherwise, you will turn them into mini-theologians. We don't need those mini-theologians around—smart people who know all the little things here and there. That doesn't help at all in their lives.

Patience and Hope

If I were to say a final word I would say that the key element for all of us dealing with life and love, is patience which is hope. In Christian terms patience is a synonym for hope. There is patience and patience. For instance the patience of somebody who in sheer resignation says, "what is the use?", and thus puts up with a situation that is not Christian. I repeat, Christian patience is a synonym for hope and hope is a synonym for faith. If we were to take a lesson from our own experience we would know that time and again in ordinary educational matters we have to wait so many years to see the fruit.

I'll never forget the case of one of my own brothers who died a few years ago. He was closest to me but older than I. As a youngster, an adolescent, he was an awful case, a real case. He drove my father crazy. Whereas the rest of the family all went through college and university, half way through high school he stubbornly decided: "I don't want to study anymore." And he really meant it. I remember my mother taunting my father, "are you going to allow him to have his way?" My father said, "What do you want me to do? To kill the boy? Because unless I kill him there is nothing we can do." So my father took him at his word and said, "What do you want?" "I want to work, to go to a factory." So he sent him to the factory to one of his friends, and everything was settled. Soon enough it became plain that the boy really was a mechanical genius. Years later, he opened his own factory. He had hundreds of workers under him, specialized engineers from all over. But anyhow, what I couldn't get over was that this man who had been the cause of almost despair to my parents, when he had his own home and children, he began to be educated by his own children. When I returned from Japan and I saw this man who was crazily busy working 20 hours a day and travelling all over the world, I couldn't believe my eyes at the transformation. And even further everytime he was in town, no matter what, he would drop everything and come daily at least to take coffee with my father. And there he was, this man whom people couldn't see at all sitting there just mesmerized by the old man, listening to him. What we all thought was lost when he was a teenager, was not wasted at all after all. But you had to wait 20 years to see the result! Haven't you seen similar cases yourself? But that waiting supposes a special type of faith—which again is love.

The person who plants the seed knows only too well that he is not throwing it away. It all appears as if he's throwing it away. As a matter of fact, should you push the question he will say, "yes, they are going to rot," as the Gospel reminds us. But what appears like waste and death, eventually will flourish into beautiful life. We don't have this type of certainty but that is why our faith has to be all the deeper and all the more grounded on God's word, for what we are doing is proclaiming the word of God. To plant the seed. To do what we can. We have to do it ungrudgingly generously. Praying and hoping that, as the psalm again has it, while we may be sowing in tears, perhaps if not we, somebody else will gather in joy someday.

Education for Faith

Alfonso M. Nebreda, S.J.

In "Education for Faith," Father Nebreda puts the question of
catechesis in schools into a wider context: that of the Church's
mission to all persons, especially as that mission is outlined in
Lumen Gentium. Again, Nebreda focuses on fundamental questions related to the call to faith. He puts the act of living faith
into its proper frame of reference: that of a personal and free
response to a loving invitation.

The reader will note how Nebreda chooses to speak of religious
education in the broader categories of communication rather
than in the narrower one of instruction or teaching. This is a
valuable perspective for those working with young people in
schools, where communication tends to be multi-dimensional,
that is, takes place at many levels in addition to that of formal
instruction. *Michael Warren*

————————————▲————————————

When we speak now of religious education it is vital to realize that we are speaking mainly in terms of the attitudinal, and
of the change in attitude which we call conversion.

Living and acting, being and doing, these are of first importance: more important than knowledge with all its verbalizing
and conceptualizing. It is not admitting the truths of faith but
rather surrendering unconditionally to God in Christ which
makes a conversion real. To be converted is to submit myself
without reservation, to God, and to commit myself, without reservation, in witness, in service, and so on. The two go together,
in a total self-donation. There are many ways of defining or

39

explaining this idea, and we could draw on many authors in the field of psychology for further explanation, but perhaps the simplest and most helpful is to refer to the Japanese way of translating attitude: *Kokoragamae*.

"How does your heart stand?" By "heart" is meant the whole personality for we do not split man up into parts. "How does your heart stand?" is not a questioning of behavior but of the total attitude, and includes everything. It suggests and hopes for a surrender to God in Christ, unconditionally, at the level of conversion, which is a very different matter from a knowledge of the truths about God and Christ. The latter would correspond to accepting a particular way of life, while the former corresponds to having a particular view of life. Ideally, the two levels should be combined. It is said that the basic root of the Sanskrit "Dharma" combines both and carries the meaning of having a view of life which becomes a way of life, so that it is unthinkable that the two could be separated. Unfortunately Western Christianity has tended to concentrate in its "religious education" on the view and so to divide faith and practice; for the Oriental this would be sheer nonsense: the Oriental understanding cannot admit the statement, "He believes but he does not practise."

It is on this whole area of the totality of conversion, the totality of commitment in faith, that we should reflect, in reference to the problems we have in religious education. In the decree of the Second Vatican Council on the Bishops' Pastoral Office in the Church, there is a very clear statement given of the aim of religious education: "Catechetical training is intended to make men's faith become living, conscious, and active, through the light of instruction" *(Christus Dominus*, n. 14).

It is obvious that instruction to knowledge is of little use without that living, conscious active faith which the decree speaks of. Ideally, knowledge of the truths of faith and conscious living of the life of faith belong together. In reality, however, they can be and are, only too often, separated.

Father Bulatao's book on "Split-Level Christianity," describes a phenomenon which is not a monopoly of the Philippines. We can find it all over the world. The split between ideas and life which faces us again and again is one of the most serious, tragic matters confronting the Church today as the Council repeatedly lamented. Ignorance in the Greek sense means absence of knowledge in the mind: in the Biblical sense, though, ignorance means a denial, a lie (cf Rom. 1:18-32). It is not an intellectual absence of knowledge. As Father Calle says in his "Catechesis for the 70's" when we speak of religious ignorance we mean absence of religious attitudes, not lack of religious knowledge.

This must be kept in mind when we come to the question of salvation. It is faith that saves, we say, whether in the baptized or the unbaptized; but if faith saves, it is not through the intellectual knowledge of the truths of faith but through the attitude of a living faith: people are saved not because of what they know or think, but because of what they do or don't do.

Any doubt about this will find its answer in the Council Documents, in the second chapter of *Lumen Gentium*, the Constitution on the Church. Paragraph 13 establishes the general fact that all men are called to be people of God; paragraphs 14 to 16 begin to treat of those who belong in some way to the Church and so are saved. If we look carefully at the categories listed there, we find that of the six categories of people mentioned only the first two consist of people who could be expected to have an intellectual knowledge of the truths of the Christian faith.

First, mention is made of the full-pledged Catholic and the catechumen, who is not-yet-baptized Catholic; then, in the second place, all other Christians. From the third category to the sixth, however there is no question of adherence to Christian tenets: the third category consists of those who share with us belief in one God, i.e., Jews and Moslems; the fourth, those whom we might call other religionists, the adherents of the great religious groups such as Buddhists, Hindus, Shintoists. The fifth category is that of the agnostic, who is not sure whether God exists or not and the sixth is that of the atheist who is convinced that there is no God.

In each case the Council says explicitly that these are people who can be saved; in stating emphatically that those of the last four groups *can* be saved the Council makes it clear that knowledge of the truths of Christianity is not essential for salvation. When we start trying to test our priorities in religious education then, we should not put the main emphasis on what is not essential, no matter what the country whether it is Australia, Japan, Hong Kong or the Philippines, or anywhere else, the same is true when it comes to this basic level.

And yet we have put and we do tend to put the greater emphasis on intellectual knowledge. Demanding as this is, it is much easier to handle: we can control intellectual knowledge; we can write a syllabus, we can measure and manipulate the content, we can check on the learning and test the memory. We try to improve methods of instruction, stimulate interest, devise and readjust. This is much easier than the extremely difficult work of reaching the heart of the person. And yet in the end we have to admit that intellectual knowledge, while it is important, no matter how complete, can never be of first importance. For unless the knowledge is constantly reflected in the whole attitude, the entire living in faith of the person, we will have a wonderful academy of mini-theologians but they are no closer to God than they were at the start, and the chances are they will not come any closer to Him in the future.

I should like at least to insert the beginning of a realization that, contrary to what we tend to think, all of us, ordinarily, intellectual knowledge will not lead to a living faith. In fact it is the very opposite that is true: living faith eventually opens the way for a true understanding of correct information. Knowing God, in the Biblical sense of "knowing" is *never* an affair of the mind. With the mind, with reason, we can analyze magnificently, but when we speak of faith we are so close to life that to analyze is to miss the essential reality.

Almost sixty years ago, Father de la Taille wrote most beautifully on the subject of prayer: "Although the light of faith resides in the mind it never enters man through the mind but through the heart." That is where we have to look for the point of entry, and that is where we have to gauge whether faith grows or diminishes. No one comes to faith or goes away from faith for reasons, in the objective sense. Rationalization will be a part of the development and the understanding but faith in a person has to be traced to the original event which today's moral theologians term the fundamental option or core decision.

Faith, we have to realize, is essentially free: a deeply personal free act from its very beginning. Unless it is free it cannot be truly human and personal, which is to say it cannot be faith. Catholic tradition, indeed, has always maintained that freedom is a basic characteristic of the act of faith. There is no question of obtaining faith by some kind of syllogistic procedure: this plus this plus this equals . . . ah, now, I see! Impossible! Faith simply is not like that.

The whole Biblical perspective of faith is so terribly different. One of the very best of today's theologians of the theology of faith, Father Alfaro, summarizes it very well. He gives the whole picture of Biblical faith as a blending of three main components: First, a knowing and an acknowledgement of Yahweh as Lord of the covenant. Man enters the realm of faith when he knows Yahweh as the Lord who forms this interpersonal bond of love with man and acknowledges him. Second, since every covenant carries an element of promise, faith explicitly or implicitly means to trust Yahweh as the Lord of the covenant, to believe in his promises. Moreover, every covenant received by man throughout the entire Old and New Testament involves obedience; the covenant implies a command and thus obedience to that command represents the third major element of biblical faith.

Now we know well that we do not spontaneously trust and obey another person. There is nothing automatic about it. To say "yes" involves the whole of ourselves. Even where the intellectual or cognitive aspect of faith is more prominent, as McKenzie points out in his Dictionary of the Bible, namely, the first of the three mentioned components—knowing and acknowledging someone is never a matter of things to be heard or nodded to apart from the total relationship adopted in regard to that very person. First and foremost is the person and the response of the heart. The fourth chapter of the first letter of John sets it out with the clarity of crystal: to know God is equivalent to loving God. Only the person who loves God knows God. There is nothing outlandish about that, we know it quite well from our own experience, from our own lives if we only stop to reflect for a moment.

Let us go back again to the problem of communication. It is comparatively easy to communicate neutral material, through objective statements which do not necessarily affect the person; but when we are treating of matters which touch the life of the person the situation is vastly different. For example, think of the whole area of politics in this country, or anywhere else, where political issues are vitally important. It is sheer nonsense to talk about being objective then: for better or for worse, as Cardinal Newman has it, you are prejudiced, meaning basically that you have made a previous judgment, just because you are who you are. It is a matter of being prejudiced rather than of having prejudices. It is the prejudice that has you, not the other way around. In one of his sermons Newman makes a statement which sounds extremely Biblical and quite avant-garde when you think of the type of theology of faith that was in vogue until recently. "Nobody can know God," he says, "unless he is or becomes prejudiced in favor of God." No one knows God, Newman is saying, unless he already has a favorable attitude to God: such a man is or is becoming Christian, whether implicitly or explicitly, and the true convert is the person who, little by little chooses to live in such a disposition. St. John tells us that no one comes to the light unless he loves the light! So, since Christ is the light, we can say that no one comes to Christ unless he loves Christ. If a person refuses to come, it is because he hates the light in some way.

These ideas are rather basic ones and are, I am sure, known to all of you, but at this time when we are making an honest attempt as educators to ask ourselves pertinent questions, it is good to discuss them again. We are certainly not suggesting that formulation and teaching of the truths of our faith has to be disregarded: not at all. What we *are* saying, though, is that this, paradoxically enough, is no truth at all for the person without the fundamental Christian attitude. Here we come to see the importance of Community, for, as Allport, one of the best American psychologists said some years ago, "Attitudes are not *taught* but *caught*." Literally caught, as something contagious is caught simply because it is carried by people or is in the very air we breathe. Entering a community with a particular attitude is like going into an air-conditioned room where the temperature is controlled: you adjust to it and your whole system becomes attuned to it to such an extent that you hardly notice it again until you walk out of it into a different atmosphere. Some of us will smile at such comparisons for we are inclined to think of this as an "anti-intellectual" approach. We forget, or we fail to realize, how deeply we are immersed in what can only be called rationalism, which is still, to a great extent, the whole pattern of thought surrounding us. Most of us really do not know how hopelessly rationalistic we are: nor do we *realize* the extent of the problems caused by our rationalism. We have made neat compartments for everything, classified and categorized them to our satisfaction and then tried to use this approach when it comes to relationships with persons. We have only to take a good look at our own everyday affairs to know that this is rather naive: there is such a difference when it comes to personal relationships, where sympathy, or empathy, becomes a major factor. If I like you, even without understanding you, I am prejudiced from the start: I will tend to agree with you and come to like you better. But if I dislike you, even if my ideas are much the same as yours, my reaction to you, if I don't take care, will be to disagree with your thinking, almost rejecting my own idea because *you* propose it. This is part of being human. Rationalism takes a man as if he were not human, tries to dissect him and pretends to be objective, which is impossible. Even in the area of physical science, when the scientist experiments he is introducing some element that was not there before and so changing somehow the conditions. Even he cannot be totally objective. How much less possibility of objectivity there is when we come to the area of the personal, which is the area of faith!

When we enter the level of persons, when we speak of faith, we can never ignore or minimize the whole atmosphere of personal prejudice, acceptance, trust, in which the key element is person to person communication: when we speak of faith touching the heart of the person we are speaking not of the emotional sensitivity of the person but of that all-pervading, total, trusting commitment which gives a transparent quality to the whole of a life. And this we cannot measure, but respect and accept in awe and thanksgiving.

Evangelization of Youth

Michael Warren

The term "evangelization" currently is being used in many different senses. The following article attempts to trace the development of evangelization theory and then apply it to youth ministry. The theory of evangelization developed by missionaries like Alfonso Nebreda does not simplify our ministry in any way. What it does do is put it on a firm foundation. The following ideas might profitably be discussed by parish councils and ministry teams to discuss the total community context of a parish's ministry to youth.

————————————— ▲ —————————————

Is this the best of times or the worst of times for leading youth to Christian faith? Some would say it is the worst of times, and to back up their position they would point to the statistics recently issued by the Department of Education at the United States Catholic Conference. Entitled, "Where Are the 6.6 Million?" this report presents some discomforting data. According to these figures, those of high school age receiving no formal religious education has risen from almost one and a half million or 36.5% in 1965 to more than three million or 61.4% in 1974. Worst-of-timers would also point out that in every diocese of the country there are parishes that have simply, and usually quietly, shut down their programs of adolescent catechesis. For these parishes the situation is so hopeless as not to be worth the effort. But, for anyone to whom the above assertions are questionable, we now have *proof* in the form of the following Greelization: "The NORC research would indicate that the various forms of non-parochial school religious instruction which have become popular in the Catholic Church in the last ten years are not an adequate substitute for parochial schools. In most cases they seem to have practically no effect at all." (*Origins*, April 8, 1976, p. 672)

Yet some others are claiming that it is the best of times for working with youth. I myself know many people working with youth, including those working in programs that supposedly "have practically no effect at all," who are finding considerable personal satisfaction in their efforts and who claim that a whole renewed ministry to youth is emerging in the American Catholic Church. More and more dioceses now have programs for training and employing young people in their early twenties as full-time youth ministers. In this country, youth retreats have never been used so widely or so well as they currently are. Some bishops will point out that in their dioceses no other area of ministry is showing the degree of creativity or the radical efforts that characterize ministry to youth.

What seems to have happened, if one may be allowed to interpret the current situation, is that work with Catholic youth, especially outside of Catholic school had indeed reached a sort of crisis of limits, an absolute low point. However, this crisis was the start of new life. When we reach a crisis point in anything— from personal life to social and political life—we are forced to reexamine fundamental principles and priorities. We are forced to search out the essential. In a crisis everything else becomes a luxury. Where ministry to youth is succeeding, it is operating from well-based fundamental principles of ministry.

In fact, one of the most valuable aspects of the current renewal of youth ministry may well be that it is uncovering principles of ministry applicable in dealing with other age groups. Radical ministry to youth, for example, has long since ceased operating on any person's *fiat*, including those of parents and pastors. Young people come together because they want to, not because they have to. They have been searched out and sounded out and invited out and then welcomed in. The day is not long off when the initiatives of youth ministers in going out to meet young people in parks, around their public schools, and at their other hang-outs will be a model for a radical ministry to religious alienated adults. Parish ministry in the future will lose much of its present character of sedentary availability and move closer to the sort of outreach ministry to which Jesus commissioned his first disciples. Youth ministers are helping us uncover the true task of ministry, as not so much one of dealing with assembled communities as one of being assemblers of the community. The task of assembling the community is basically the task of evangelization.

The new dynamism of renewed ministries in the Catholic Church, including ministry to youth, was foreshadowed almost a quarter century ago in Europe. In fact, the situation out of which the word "evangelization" grew twenty-five years ago is strikingly similar to that out of which contemporary youth ministry is growing. Understanding this similarity will be helpful toward understanding other relationships between youth ministry and evangelization.

After World War II Europe seemed to be in a desperate situation as regards the Christian churches, including the Catholic Church. Catholic missionaries being trained in France to spread the gospel in mission lands came to see that many "Christians" in Europe had been baptized and instructed but had never come to conversion to the Way of Jesus. Europe itself was as much a mission territory as the so-called pagan lands. The religious affiliation of the non-converted Christians had been socially induced but never personally ratified. In fact, Alfonso Nebreda came to see that it was easier to lead to Christ a Japanese who knew little of the gospel than it was to lead a French Catholic who reacted to the same message with a stifled yawn.

These missionaries, under the direction of their teacher, Dominican theologian Andre Liege, began to distinguish between catechesis and evangelization. Catechesis was a process of leading both communities and individual members of the faithful (i.e., of the faith-filled) to maturity of faith. Catechesis, then, dealt with those who had been converted to Jesus. The pre-conversion process of proclaiming the gospel and leading people to faith in Jesus demanded a new term and a more radical frame of mind. For the new term, Liege suggested the word "evangelization," that is "gospelling," or even "good-newsing." Evangelization demanded a missionary attitude. Indeed those who studied with Liege, even if like Pierre Babin they remained in France, maintained a pastoral attitude that was basically a missionary one. It is no wonder then, that so many of the statements on current youth ministry, like the soon-to-be-released statement of the USCC, echo so many of the concerns of Liege's Evangelization School of more than two decades ago.

What, then, are these concerns on which youth ministry in this country is based and which are so close to the concerns of evangelization? Because of the limitations of space, I will examine two that are of key importance: concern for clear witness and concern for indigenization.

One of the preoccupations of literature dealing with evangelization is a concern with signs and ultimately with the sign of witness. At a time when the Church in Europe seemed to be dying because many persons were Christian in name only, such a concern with witness was needed. The personal lives of man showed few signs of fidelity to the gospel of Jesus. Thus the Roman Catholic Church and the other Christian churches were found to be severely lacking in credibility. As groups of persons supposedly committed to Jesus' Way, their personal and corporate lives were not believable.

Far from being limited to European catechists in the 1950's, this preoccupation with the lived life of a community as a key source of its credibility characterized the earliest Christian communities in the New Testament. Scholars point out that the word used for preaching the gospel among the first disciples of Jesus was *kerussein* or "to preach." Once communities were more solidly established, another word began to be used. It seems that when the churches secured a foothold in society, the gospelling of individual preachers was not of itself sufficient. The churches themselves had to be signs of the good news. The new word was *matturein*, meaning "to witness." Thus the later Johannine writings prefer the word "witness," suggesting a more communitarian dimension of the task of proclaiming the gospel. By the time of John, those to whom the gospel had been preached had become established as communities of believers, and their task was one of taking care that their corporate life be a clear sign. In the context of John, then, witness suggests a corporate form of preaching. The community's life of communion and fellowship was to be a powerful word, making believable their commitment to the gospel.

In a quick overview of the literature of contemporary youth ministry, one finds much attention to the importance of communitarian witness. Those working with the young point again and again to the importance for young people of a fellowship of adult believers whose corporate life reflects the gospel in deed and not just in word. Personal and corporate credibility is a powerful positive force in the lives of the young. On the other hand, parish life that is a mere going through the paces and where the gospel has been domesticated if not caged, seems to many young people astonishingly incredible.

Admittedly this is a difficult issue to face, since it suggests that the evangelization of young people cannot succeed fully without a more gospel-centered life on the part of whole parishes. Moreover all will admit that such a re-conversion process is not an easy one to effect, even if all could agree on the new orientation that would be called for. Many youth ministers will claim they are simply trying to do the possible "in forming smaller fellowship groups comprised of a majority of young people and a minority of adults struggling to deepen their own commitment to Jesus and His Way. One can find these groups on youth retreat weekends and in Sunday youth liturgies attended by large numbers of young people in Catholic high school and college chapels.

Those directing such community-centered programs are aware that a future problem will be finding adult communities, especially parishes, which these young people can eventually join. Many of these leaders will apologize for what is an apparent alienation from parish life by claiming they are attempting not the ideal but more an expedient called for by the times. However they can take heart that their efforts seem to be following the lines elaborated by the recent Apostolic Exhortation of Pope

Paul on Evangelization. By trying to establish core groups of believers to which others can affiliate more or less closely, they are undertaking an effective evangelization of young people.

Above all the gospel must be proclaimed by witness. Take a Christian or a handful of Christians who, in the midst of their own community, show their capacity for understanding and acceptance, their sharing of life and destiny with other people, their solidarity with the efforts of all for whatever is noble and good.

Let us suppose that, in addition, they radiate in an altogether simple and unaffected way their faith in values that go beyond current values, and their hope in something that is not seen and that one would not dare to imagine. Through this wordless witness these Christians stir up irresistible questions in the hearts of those who see how they live: Why are they like this? Why do they live in this way? What or who is it that inspires them? Why are they in our midst? Such a witness is already a silent proclamation of the good news and a very powerful and effective one. Here we have an initial act of evangelization (par. 21).

One could theorize that the eventual conversion of many nominally-Christian adults will take place by means of the witness of these smaller communities-within-communities, which seem to have such an influence now in the lives of the young.

For all ages it is true that adherence to the gospel cannot remain abstract and unincarnated but it must at some point become embodied and concretized by a visible entry into a community of believers.

Another concern of youth ministry that is closely connected with evangelization is indigenization. Although many ministering to youth are unfamiliar with the somewhat awkward term, "indigenization," yet the meaning behind this word guides much of the best thinking in youth ministry today. Thus a brief examination of indigenization is in order here.

For many decades now, much of the so-called "new catechetics" could be summed up in the word "adaptation." The word of God is a word for man, and must be proclaimed in such a way that it connects with a person's own life. Following this insight through to its logical conclusions has triggered vast changes in the way the ministry of the word is undertaken. Catechists have taken keen interest in the various social sciences, as one step in uncovering the mentalities of those to whom they wish to proclaim the gospel. Stages of psychological development got special attention in an attempt to help others grow in their understanding of the Christian message. Catechists questioned many practices taken for granted in the past, particularly the practice of having children memorize theological propositions they could not possibly understand and could very probably misunderstand. In a sense, then, adaptation looks at the matter of communicating the gospel from the point of view of the communicator. Adaptation is the task of the communicator, who must take pains to tailor the gospel to particular mentalities.

Indigenization, however, has moved the question of adaptation to a new depth, to a new level of seriousness. This term suggests that the good news can and must come to grow in the life of a people. The gospel is meant for all soils. It is meant to be a native flower wherever it is sown. Whereas adaptation suggests a transplant, that is, something living in non-native soil, indigenization suggests the process by which Christianity takes root totally in the unique soil and atmosphere of a particular culture or mentality. Whereas adaptation is done by those who receive the gospel themselves. It can be only encouraged by ministers of the word, with the actual process happening among the people.

The strongest recent pressure for indigenization has come from India, struggling to find, at the end of a long period of colonial rule and of aping Western customs, the forms of Christian living natural to the gospel in their culture. Indian catechetical leaders realize that many Indians will not be able to recognize the gospel call except in Indian dress. For these theologians, a prime analogue of indigenization is the Incarnation. Indigenization is much more in line with the Incarnation than is adaptation. Jesus came as a native. As exegete Raymond Brown is so fond of saying, "He was a Galilean Jew of the first third of the first century." If Jesus came as a native, then the good news is meant to go native wherever it goes.

In youth ministry, the gospel-gone-native can be seen in many developments, one of the chief being the new sense of ministry taking root among young people themselves. Where once young people showed in response to the gospel a desire for apostolic action of various kinds, today's young people in addition are asking to exercise a direct ministry in the Church. In some dioceses, college grads are being trained as youth ministers and assuming full-time positions ministering to either their peers or to those just younger. High school aged young people are now serving as leaders on retreat teams. In some cases, the adults who direct them recognize them as the most effective members of these teams. In some places, teens are now training to develop the skills for various peer ministries, including peer counseling.

Another form of indigenization in youth ministry is youth liturgies. Matteo Ricci, the Jesuit refused permission to allow the 17th century Chinese to develop their own native forms of Christian worship, would be pleased at the reverent and appropriate liturgical forms being developed by young people. These forms are expressive of the entire mentality of young people. For instance, these liturgies use a variety of strategies to allow each person to have her/his own say in response to the scripture readings. Such responsiveness is important to young people groping to discover their own word of faith. Subgroups work to prepare appropriate mime, dance, and musical responses within the Eucharist. Black and hispanic teens are finding ways to express both their own youth culture and their ethnic riches in worship. Our national liturgical scene is being enriched by these efforts.

Such developments are threatening to parish leaders who wonder if the young will ever return to parish assemblies from these more "native" liturgies. The more accurate question might be whether parish assemblies will welcome some of the native riches of young people and in this way allow them the influence they are denied in most parishes. Youth ministry today is enfranchising young people, giving them a vote and a say and a task and a ministry. Although young people need the sort of intergenerational contact available in parish life, one wonders if they will ever get it unless parishes on their own part are willing to seek out and recognize the gifts of the young.

Again, this aspect of youth ministry is summed up in another passage from Pope Paul's Exhortation:

> The gospel, and therefore evangelization, are certainly not identified with culture, and they are independent in regard to all cultures. Nevertheless, the kingdom which the Gospel proclaims is lived by men who are profoundly linked to a culture and the building up of the Kingdom cannot avoid borrowing the elements of human culture or cultures. Though independent of cultures, the gospel and evangelization are not necessarily incompatible with them; rather they are capable of permeating them all without becoming subject to any one of them.
>
> The split between the gospel and culture is without a doubt the drama of our time, just as it was of other times. Therefore every effort must be made to ensure a full evangelization of culture, or more correctly of culture (par. 20).

Pope Paul, summing up reflections of the catechetical community on evangelization over twenty years, is affirming something that good youth ministers have been putting into practice for many years now. Before one can speak to a particular culture, one must know it, be familiar with it. One must attend to it, in the sense of paying attention to it and spending time trying to understand it. Youth ministry does not wish to affirm every aspect of youth culture, but it is serious about understanding all aspects. Youth ministers worthy of their calling listen to young people, listen to their music, attend the movies they find significant, read their magazines and their novels. Such ministers to youth are constantly preparing themselves for speaking out of youth culture and not at it.

One can hope that youth ministry will continue to grow in coming years and that many will continue to select it as an area of specialized ministry. One can also hope that some of those who have had success in youth ministry will begin giving more attention to an area of ministry long neglected and in desperate need of fulltime specialists. That area is ministry to the young adult.

For many years now there has been in the United States a network of persons ministering to young adults—but only if they happened to be on college campuses. Our bias in the Catholic Church has been toward those in schools and colleges, a bias that seems to lurk unconsciously in Greeley's latest assertions about contemporary Catholic life in the U.S. Yet there are many thousands of Catholic young people who elect not to go to college but who move into various kinds of employment, working in offices and department stores or in garage grease pits and short order kitchens.

These young people have religious needs like everyone else, but somehow they seem to have disappeared from our parish assemblies, especially in the big cities. There is little hard data on the 18-25 year-olds and their attitudes toward established Churches, possibly because it is difficult to locate them. They seem to disappear into their jobs and their singles apartments and their scattered hang-outs. The churches are not going to find them neatly assembled together on college campuses. If there is going to be ministry to the young adult, if we are going to find out what their religious and other human needs are, these persons must be sought out through the hard work of dedicated ministers.

Ministry to young adults will have to find these young people where they are. In cities like New York that ministry will involve attention to the various watering places where this group comes together on weekends, night spots with names like The Brass Onion, Shenanigans, The Players, and so forth. If one could make projections from what is currently going on in youth ministry, the key to young adult ministry will lie in calling young adults to ministry to their own peers. After all they know the places, the people and the problems. They also have the maturity needed for serious ministry.

Working at the national level to lay a groundwork for more

attention to young adults is Father Patrick O'Neil, representative at the United States Catholic Conference for both campus ministry and ministry to young adults not on campuses. As a first step in encouraging greater focus on young adults, Father O'Neil has convened a Working Board on Ministry to Young Adults. Made up of a dozen persons associated with various aspects of youth ministry throughout the country, this group has committed itself to eight meetings over a two-year period, in an effort to determine some first steps in establishing ministries to young adults in various dioceses.

Outcomes of these initiatives are still unclear. Serious attention to this neglected area will not happen overnight. Whatever happens will, like youth ministry, follow sound principles of evangelization, like witness and indigenization. Ministers to young adults will have the joy of learning by doing. May they find joy in small accomplishments.

Catholic Education
as Evangelization

José M. Calle

José Calle, of the East Asian Pastoral Institute in the Philippines, offers a challenge to all those who would minister to young people within the context of a Catholic school. According to Calle's vision, a credible attempt to lead young people in Catholic high schools deeper into the mystery of faith involves an effort better coordinated and more total than that suggested by individual religion teachers preoccupied only with teaching their own classes. Calle's program suggests that the matter of evangelization cannot be left to the religion department alone but must be the task of an entire faculty and administration. Calle's vision is both realistic and demanding.

Although this article specifically addresses faith development in the context of a school, much of what is said is applicable to a variety of catechetical programs for young people outside of school contexts. Those working with youth retreat programs and with any of the varied non-school catechetical approaches now being experimented with will profit from reflecting on Father Calle's evangelizing catechesis.　　　　*Michael Warren*

------------------ ▲ ------------------

In the context of exploring the real aims and objectives of our Catholic high schools, it seems of paramount importance to ask ourselves what unique contribution Catholic high schools can offer to education. What is specifically unique and typical of our education; what makes it Catholic and Christian? We would like to attempt an answer to this question by sharing with you a personal conviction that has grown over the years of involvement with educators and pastoral theologians.

Catholic-Christian education, to preserve its identity, must be essentially a process of Evangelization. This would seem to be unique in Christian education compared with other non-Christian educational ventures.

What Do We Mean by a Process of Evangelization?

In the proposed draft for the next Synod of Bishops on the Evangelization of the Modern World, it is plainly admitted that "the word 'evangelization' is commonly understood in several different senses today." In concrete the document mentions four:

1. Evangelization is every activity whereby the world is in any way transformed in accordance with the will of God.

2. Evangelization is the priestly, prophetic and royal activity whereby the Church is built up according to Christ's intention.

3. Evangelization is the first proclamation of the Gospel to non-Christians.

4. Evangelization is the activity whereby the Gospel is proclaimed and explained, and whereby living Faith is awakened in non-Christians and fostered in Christians.

The aims of these various notions of Evangelization appear to be respectively: (1) Transformation of the World; (2) Building of the Kingdom; (3) Conversion to Christ; (4) Living Faith. With regard to the activities by which these aims are to be attained, the third and fourth notions seem to limit themselves to preaching and teaching; the second emphasizes the specific ecclesial activities, while the first notion includes secular activities as well.

In any case it is right to say that "these various meanings are so closely interconnected that the activities they signify cannot be properly separated" (Synod of Bishops on the Evangelization of the Modern World, p. 1).

We would like to put forward a few observations concerning these notions of Evangelization.

First, we must state positively that they are very traditional and theologically sound. They remind us of those essential elements of Evangelization without which it ceases to be Evangelization. They describe very well Evangelization as a privileged ecclesial function.

On the other hand we cannot ignore the fact that such an ecclesial function is essentially "educational"; and that our present concern is how to fulfill effectively this educational function among contemporary men. Contemporary man is therefore the receiver, the subject of Evangelization. It is sound pedagogy to know who he is. This is not the place to draw his complete profile, but just to sketch a few traits that are of special interest at the moment. First of all contemporary man is not inclined to learn by listening silently to one person. He learns more effectively by "searching" and discovering together with other persons. Secondly his focus of attention is the world of interpersonal realities with all its mystery and complexity. Thirdly he grows and changes by finding for his own inner yearnings and aspirations ever more meaning and finality. Lastly, his key question, when confronted with Christianity, is simply this: What can Christ and Christianity add to my humanness?

Our assumption is that Evangelization, as an educational function, has to pay serious attention to this mental and psychological make-up of those being evangelized. We cannot see how the aims of Evangelization, such as transformation of the world, building the kingdom, conversion to Christ, and living Faith can be achieved otherwise. We all agree, of course, that in the final instance all of this is the work of God. But the question here is what kind of vision and praxis of Evangelization should we have so that our task, as human instruments of God's grace, may be more in accordance with the work of the Spirit in the hearts of contemporary men?

Pondering all this we were brought to elaborate a vision and a praxis of Evangelization that may sound new, but does not in fact exclude any of the essential elements of the other notions of Evangelization.

When addressing Catholic educators, we should say, that catholic christian education, to preserve its identity, must be essentially a process of Evangelization. We understand it as follows: The process of Evangelization is *the collective search for the ultimate meaning of the mystery of man in the light of the mystery of Christ.*

We shall comment briefly on the key-elements of this definition, and its implications for the work of Catholic educators.

Collective Search

With the word "collective" we want to suggest the idea that Evangelization, as a process, is not something that we simply do *for* others, but something that must be done *with* others. To create this attitude of "with-otherness," important changes have to be made in the usual network of relationships between teachers and students, between preachers and catechumens. I am referring to a pattern of relationships where one person plays the role of knowing everything, and the others the role of knowing nothing, one possesses the truth, and the others receive it, one talks and the others listen, one is superior and the others inferior. Evangelization demands quite another type of interpersonal relationships through which everyone both students and teachers, may grow in mutual trust, understanding, respect, shared reverence and humility. Any manifestation of arrogance on the part of those who are in the position of teachers, is obviously fatal.

In other words what the process of Evangelization normally needs is a *community* (no matter how embryonic it may be), a community of persons who set out to search *together*. This is the vital milieu of that deeper level of interpersonal *communication* whether it be of teachers with students or of teachers or students among themselves; in which change of attitudes and change of values can take place.

The Council has a statement that is appropriate here: "Christians are joined with the rest of men in the search for truth, and for the genuine solution to the numerous problems which arise in the life of individuals and from social relationships" (*Gaudium et Spes*, n. 16).

This search for truth is a life-long task. Our students should not leave our schools thinking they possess the whole truth, the complete answer. If they leave us with the realization that they have to continue searching, if they see us and hear us, humbly and without pretence walking along with them, searching too, day by day, for the rest of our lives, they have in the concrete the reality of that continuous conversion, that continuing change of attitude, essential to the life-long search we have been speaking of.

Ultimate Meaning

We are not talking about the superficial meaning of things and events but the deep meaning, not the partial meaning of reality but the total meaning of it, not the provisional meaning but the ultimate. The word meaning has many connotations but first of all it indicates *that which makes life worthwhile.*

The human person, complicated animal that he is, cannot survive as a person without meaning. This is what the Catholic institution should be able to provide as its contribution to civilization. If our schools do not lead people to this collective search for ultimate meaning then we might as well close them. No matter how many graduates come from the school, no matter how high their degrees and how well placed they may find themselves, if they have not found meaning in their lives we have been wasting our time. Saying this in reference to Evangelization we mean to refer not only to Catholic institutions in Catholic countries but to Christian institutions in any country or any culture.

Mystery of Man

We are speaking of the ultimate meaning of the *mystery of man.* We should not fool around with any other reality when this remains the essential field of research and of action. The gospel is the good news for *man* in reference to this mystery of our human existence. Whatever news we preach about the truths of faith, if it is not presented in relation to this, to the ultimate meaning of the mystery of man, it is not good news at all. The whole reality of salvation is meant to give ultimate meaning to the mystery of man.

What do we mean when we say "the mystery of man"? If we try to fabricate some kind of a definition we run the risk of destroying the very mystery. It is the very life of man, the dynamic reality of all those inner forces that make us man, by which we are sure that we are not wood, or stone, or animal. It has to do with the complex network of energies, needs and aspirations so interrelated that to speak of a few is in some way to consider them all. The need, for example, to love and be loved, the need to understand and be understood; the need to reach out to others and cooperate with them; the need to be responsible to our own conscience, to our society, to our culture. The impulse to search for meaning in the very physical existence we have, the demand to find hope in confrontation with the mystery of the reality of death. All of these are elements of the mystery of man. To all of these we have to try to bring an ultimate meaning and our whole educational process should be geared to a collective search for this.

In the Light of the Mystery of Christ

We refer this to Evangelization, knowing that in our search the ultimate meaning will be found in the light of the mystery of Christ. One statement of the Council which we as Catholic educators should never forget is this: "The truth is that only in the mystery of the incarnate Word does the mystery of man take on light. For Christ, the final Adam, fully reveals man to man himself and makes his supreme calling clear" (cf. also *Gaudium et Spes*, nn. 15, 11, 18, 19, 22).

This is the kerygma of the Apostles, articulated now by the apostles of the Second Vatican Council, in its up-to-date 20th-century expression. These declarations of the Council imply that the religion teacher in a Catholic educational institution is first and foremost a prophet of meaning: not in the sense of telling or foretelling future events, but in the sense of being able to interpret the realities in the lives of people and bring to light their ultimate meaning, in the light of the Mystery of Christ. In this regard Catholic educators must try to be explicit as possible, *provided* they have the wisdom to realize that, when dealing with students living in a non-Christian culture, *verbal* explicitations may not help, but may actually hinder the action of the Spirit who has a more subtle, hidden and mysterious way of bringing about salvation in their hearts.

By Developing Consciousness and Awareness of Life Experiences

Communication keeps recurring as one of our main concerns, one of our worries, maybe, because, after all, Evangelization is essentially communication, as preaching is, as teaching is. If we do not communicate, then there is no teaching, nor preaching, nor evangelization. This is worth thinking about at length, for we may find we are talking to ourselves! How are we going to make communication effective, then? When you reflect on your own task as educators you soon realize that there is effective communication when you *say the right thing at the right time in the right way.* That sounds so obvious that there is a danger of taking it as a mere platitude. Until you start to ask "What is the *right thing?*"

In our context the *right thing* has to be something having a bearing on the here and now *experience,* or the *environment,* of the listener. Anything else might be memorized, put into the mental filing system for use at examinations, treated as information, but the giving of information is by no means the whole of effective communication! Good pedagogy makes it necessary to make use of the experience of the environment of the person in the process of Evangelization. We should never be afraid of appealing to personal experience, personal awareness of the environment, because it is this that ensures effective communication.

This is the pedagogical reason for our insistence on *experiential methodology.* When the awareness of people is awakened, when they are conscious of their experiences, their aspirations and yearnings, and when we too are conscious of the aspirations and yearnings of the people whom we wish to serve, the people with and for whom we live, these become the spring-board of our Evangelization. The aspirations and yearnings of people are, of course, conditioned by the environment.

We have to realize that no liturgical programs, no matter how well prepared, no Bible study programs, no matter how good, and no new theological syllabus, no matter how up-to-date, will ever, of themselves, solve the problems of effective Evangelization. They must be integrated into a program and a process of Evangelization through which the whole community is alive in their own collective search. They must search together for the ultimate meaning of the mystery of man, their own mystery, in the light of the mystery of Christ. They will do this through a continual awareness and pondering of their own life-experiences, in reference to their own socio-cultural, political or religious environment.

With these brief reflections we tried simply to draw out the pastoral implications and pedagogical applications of the Theology of Revelation, the Theology of Faith and the Theology of the Mission of the Church, as they are understood today in the light of the Council. We find in them the theological rationale of a process of Evangelization that is altogether experiential, environmental and *communitarian*.

Social Processes
in Adolescent Catechesis

Michael Warren

The following article has an interesting history. It grew out of actual experience of ministering to young people in parishes and out of a conviction that many programs for teens fail because they are not attuned to the mentality and needs of the young. They are serving the needs of adults rather than those of young people. In trying out various initiatives with older teens at the parish level, the writer found the community or interaction dimension to be the key one. The very same thing had been true of his experience as a teacher in Catholic high schools. Experience with young people in various settings over a number of years seemed to be saying: Attend first to the way young people come together. To neglect this aspect is to invite disaster.

The notes were added later in an attempt to show that attention to the "interaction dimension" is not an easily dismissed frill in youth programs. Catechetical, educational, and social theory and research back up many of the claims of this article, which are applicable to a wide range of programs for young people.

──────────────── ▲ ────────────────

In the summer of 1969, a rather odd incident occurred that might well shed light on the direction religious education should take in the 70's. A telecast of the spectacular Apollo 11 flight to the moon was broken by a news report of the Harlem Folk Festival, an all-day program devoted to Black Culture. As the news reporter interviewed about a dozen of the rapt participants in the Festival, it was quite clear that they considered man's race to the moon irrelevant. Their attention that hot July afternoon was so fixed on their soul music that several even scorned the reporter's questions, ignoring him as if he had been hopelessly rude and insensitive in interrupting their enjoyment of the Festival with his silly questions about the moon flight. Others, more vocal and more militant, explicitly stated that their concern that afternoon was the black man's identity, not the white man's technological triumphs. It was an ironical situation: as millions around the world focused in fascination on man's conquest of outer space, here was a group focusing with even more interest on man's inner space. They had no interest in the moon. They were intent on exploring the inner space of their own black culture, of their own personal group identity.

An authentic parallel might be drawn between what is going on today in the black community and adolescents' attempts to achieve self-identity. And just as the black community of Harlem was attempting to establish its personal identity through group participation in a celebration of its own culture, so most teenagers achieve personal identity, to a large extent at least, through the mediation of groups. The purpose of this paper is to consider the importance of the group process for the catechesis of teenagers, with particular focus on what could be called the process of socialization in the catechesis of the young, that is, on the social processes that are at least part of the vehicle of catechesis.[1]

In one sense, we are all aware of the social groupings and their influence: family groups, peer groups, church groups, and so forth. The existence of these groupings has been stressed for so many decades now that their existence seems obvious. In another sense, however, most of us are but marginally aware of the pervasive influence of these groupings and their interaction.[2] For the catechist, these groupings must cease to be a mere fact and become instead a task, i.e., an object of constant reflection and attention. For the adolescent, group influences have a special power that must be reckoned with in a catechetical program. A more sophisticated understanding of these group influences might encourage us to stop attempting the impossible: theology on a fifty-minutes-a-week basis or the serious probing of dilemmas of Christian existence at one week intervals. It would be better to "wind down" our attempts a bit and allow for less grim purposefulness and more informality, less fixation on academic content and more attention to the context or environment of these programs.[3]

For the purposes of this paper, we will focus on the group process as it affects especially the faith formation of teenagers.[4] In treating this topic, the following four points will be considered: (1) teenagers need groups; (2) teenagers need to feel relaxed in groups; (3) relaxed groupings of teenagers are where they tend to become Church; (4) in the light of these considerations, a new look at the question of content for this age group is needed.

Teenagers Need Groups

This statement means that teenagers need all kinds of groups if they are to achieve self-identity. They need formal groups that have their own unbudging norms, to which one must adjust if one is to remain a group member. A school band would be one such formal group, but there are dozens of possibilities here. Other groups combine aspects of formality and informality; persons must adjust to others but also they can expect that others will adjust to them. The family group is an example of this type. Most families with teenagers are engaged in a sort of psychic tug-of-war in which each must adjust to the pressures of the others. These family tensions can be healthy for a teenager trying to define himself, though at the same time they will probably be painful for parents who tend to get tired of digging their heels in and tugging on that rope. To repeat: these tensions can be creative. John W. Gardner suggests that family relationships provide both creative tensions and models with which the young identify.

Young people do not assimilate the values of their group by learning the words (truth, justice, etc.) and their definitions.

They learn attitudes, habits and ways of judging. They learn these in intensely personal transactions with their immediate family or associates. They learn them in the routines and crises of living, but they also learn them through songs, stories, drama and games. They do not learn ethical principles; they emulate ethical (or unethical) people. They do not analyze or list the attributes they wish to develop; they identify with people who seem to them to have these attributes. That is why young people need models, both in their imaginative life and in their environment, models of what man at his best can be.[5]

However, an adolescent also needs those highly informal groups where oneself and one's peers themselves establish the norms and the rituals and the structure of the group. These are the groups that congregate after school, at the local hamburger stands, in garages where guitar and singing groups work out their new rhythms and their perennial songs of love and loneliness. These informal groups or cliques can be quite rigid, as any teenager who has been made to feel excluded from them can tell you.

Adolescents often behave much like members of an old-fashioned aristocracy. They are extremely conservative in their dress and tastes, but the conventions to which they adhere are purely those of their own social group; they try to ignore the demands of the larger society if these conflict with their own.[6]

Teenagers need groups, then, and in fact, several different kinds of groups exist to which they belong. But we need to go further and ask about the interaction of these different groupings.[7] A parish in New York provides an illustration of the possible catechetical significance of such interaction. For two years it was almost impossible to get the older high school students of that parish to come for religious instruction. The catechists tried everything: tri-semesters, small classes, classes in the home, and even the miracle drug of the religious education world, films.

They explored the whole range of options, but to no avail, even though they were a superior group of teachers. The young people still came mainly under some sort of duress. The parents drove them to class and waited until they had at least entered the building before driving off. And yet, in the same parish, the older teenagers who scorned the parish religion program went willingly to a nondenominational program called Young Life.[8] Some teachers decided to investigate. By attending Young Life sessions and talking with the students informally, they found out that the Young Life director had spent a great deal of time around the local high school and had penetrated some of the informal groups to which the young people belonged. They had come to know him in informal situations. As a result, it was socially acceptable among them to attend Young Life, while at the same time those who were forced to attend CCD were ridiculed as being "out of it" or as being overly dominated by their parents.

Whether the young people were right or wrong in their view of the situation is immaterial here. The point is that this was how they perceived their parish religion program, and their perception was creating a class atmosphere of hostility among the students and frustration among the teachers. The situation was finally resolved when the teachers modified their program in order to incorporate some of the informality of the Young Life program *and* when they began having much more informal contact with the students. (At least one sign that their efforts so far have begun to pay off is that the students occasionally bring their Protestant friends for a session.)

The focus in religious education used to be on the matter to be learned.[9] This was supreme, and religious education was all about getting the facts across to students. Then the focus shifted to the individuals being catechized. It was recognized that one must start with them and adapt the message to their level of intellectual and emotional development. Gone were the harsh methods used to impose mastery of catechism answers in morning memory sessions. Instead, enlightened catechists all read up on psychology and on educational theory so as to better understand how to bring about a meeting of mind and matter. Now, however, we have to move another step. We have to become much more aware of the total environment of our teaching including both the physical environment and the persons concerned.[10] Every group itself is a content, teaching constantly and subtly, communicating a message that everyone in the group is picking up.

This subtle group "content" is well illustrated by a group of eighth grade parochial school boys who somehow decided that religion was strictly for girls. Just how they came to this conclusion is not essential to our concern here. The fact remained that this was how all the boys in the class viewed the matter. It became an accepted thing that the boys just did not participate in religion class, at least did not volunteer answers or ask questions. Any boy who ignored this convention heard about it after class or got a withering look from his friends right there in the classroom.

The teacher fell right into the trap. She directed most of her attention to the girls. After all, they were the willing participants, the interested ones. Thus, the more the girls participated to the exclusion of the boys, the more the boys became convinced that religion was, in fact, for girls, since the girls were the only ones who showed any interest in class. Near the end of the school year, the teacher happened to mention to a catechetical consultant that boys do not care about their faith, whereas girls are very interested. But the consultant knew that eighth grade boys are just as interested in religious questions as are eighth grade girls, and if they appear not to be, there must be a reason.[11] In this case at least, the group process would not allow the boys to express openly their interest. The teacher unwittingly had been fostering a group attitude which, for half the group at least, was working against all her efforts to lead the children to Christ. The hidden group content among the boys was in direct conflict with that class' religion lessons. Unfortunately, it was too close to the end of the year to resolve the problem satisfactorily, but a beginning was made by holding separate religion classes for the boys.

Hervé Carrier addresses himself to this whole area of the influence of group identification on religious education in his excellent study, *The Sociology of Religious Belonging*.

Perhaps at the psychological level it would be found that the religious feeling of the young who leave the Church so soon after their First Holy Communion had never been firmly related to the ecclesiastical group itself. The hypothesis merits testing by empirical methods. Would there not be found, in this line of research, one of the more profound causes of youth's religious separation? And if we confronted these observations with those we have already made about the influence of secular reference groups, we would probably understand how spiritual adhesions are strengthened or dissolved on the psychosociological level. We would also learn how the young are often psychologically and morally divided between groups based on family ties, school, friends, leisure, the neighborhood, apprenticeship, etc. Each of these groups imposes its values, norms, rewards, and sanctions. We could legitimately suspect that in a great number of cases, if the competition among these groups operates to the detriment of religious fidelity, it is because institutional transfer operates toward the church, and subsequent psychological reference lacked consistency and true personal meaning for the practicing youngster.[12]

Carrier is maintaining that it is quite possible that a youngster identify with various subgroups and against the Church. He can develop loyalties to various groups that will not allow him to be attached to the Church. Those concerned with the religious education of adolescents must become more keenly aware of these group influences before they will be able to develop strategies to deal with them and possibly offset them. These strategies are not strategies for domination or manipulation but rather strategies to foster young people's freedom from oppressive group pressures and also the opportunity to develop the religious dimension of their lives.

Teenagers Need To Feel Relaxed in Groups

A second point is that teenagers need to feel relaxed in groups—in *some* groups, though obviously not in all. This is a necessity because the adolescent has a confused social role to play.[13] While both the child and the adult have a clearly defined role in life, the adolescent is in the peculiarly awkward situation of stepping from one role into the other. One is not a child nor an adult; actually the young person is some of both. One feels this way about oneself, and it is no wonder society treats the young person in an ambiguous manner. But it is among one's peers, who share this ambiguous situation, that a person can feel most at home. We have all met concerned parents who complain of their teenage daughter: "She's living in her own little world." Well, such behavior is not untypical and not necessarily bad in all instances. Their own little world may be necessary to them for a while.[14] It is a place where they can ask their man-child questions and live with their man-child frustrations.[15]

Now if it is true that young people need groups that allow them to relax, this is especially true if they are to look at themselves and learn about themselves. Admittedly, there are many different levels of relaxation appropriate to different kinds of learning situations. By the word "relaxed" is not meant a state of casual inattention or undisciplined informality, but rather a situation where tensions are not blocking learning. A general rule might be formulated as follows: the more personal the content to be learned or dealt with, the more relaxed the learning situation must be.

The kind of religious learning appropriate to the teenager is highly personal. Teenagers are radical personalizers. That is why it is so easy to hurt their feelings. That is also why they are not much interested in learning just factual material about their religion. Their concern tends to be their faith, that is, religion as it is personalized in their everyday lives. The teenager is engaged in a search for his own identity and for his own faith as part of that identity. We are now realizing that one cannot separate the two, and consequently, the newer religion materials are concerned

with many different aspects of the lives of teenagers: their songs,
their social concerns, their view of other people, and so forth.[16]
All these concerns are tied in with faith. In order to be able to
consider these matters, in order to be able to think deeply about
them, the teenagers must be relaxed.[17] This is a fact of life, and
is just as true of adults as it is of adolescents. How many adults
would be willing to discuss their faith in a deeply personal way
unless they felt comfortable and assured that their self-revela-
tions would not be used against them. To repeat: teenagers need
to feel relaxed in groups, and this is especially true of their
religious education groups.

Where Teenagers Become Church

Thirdly, relaxed groupings of teenagers are where they become Church. They become Church in a theological sense and in
a sociological sense. If teenagers are to become a community
joined in a common shared faith in the presence of the Risen
Lord—that is, if they are to become Church—they will generally
—though, of course, there can be many exceptions—achieve this
consciously shared faith only by a great deal of dialogue and
openness and sharing. How does one know he shares a value
with a person unless they have talked about it together? Unless
teenagers are led to share their faith with one another and come
to see that Christ is acting in their lives, it is hard to see that they
will ever want to celebrate that common faith joyfully in the
Eucharist. And once they do share their common faith with one
another, it is hard to see how they could keep from wanting to
share the Eucharist together.

Of course, they do not come to this sharing of common
faith on their own; they need adults who will be willing to share
their own faith with them and who will allow them to express
their own groping and wobbly faith openly. In recruiting catechists for teenagers, in fact, it would be preferable to have a relatively uneducated person who is willing to share his faith than a
gold mine of theological distinctions who keeps this faith under a
bushel. One of the insights of the sociology of religion is that the

man of faith tends to beget faith in others, who then form a community of faith. Pierre Babin puts is this way:

> If young people are to climb successfully the slope of adolescence, they must have before their eyes the living evidence that they can serve God without turning their back on life. They need to see concrete instances of men and women who are fully human as well as fully Christian. And they must also find support in flexible structures that are adapted to our time (school, youth group, and atmosphere of friendship). When this is the case, when they have the benefit of a Christian environment that is open and missionary in spirit, when they are in touch with adults in whom they recognize a deep humanity as well as a living faith, then their spiritual life will develop and unfold quite naturally. They will readily take their place in the life of a fraternal community.[18]

However, there is another sense in which relaxed groupings of teenagers become Church. After all, adolescents are humiliated at being identified with children, and do not yet have adult status. As children they were herded into church and had no say about it; as adults they will have definite status and responsibility in the Church, especially in the post-Vatican II Church. However adolescents tend to find few points for identification with the Church. Often young people find themselves members of a Church that expects full fidelity from them, but which gives them little say and makes little effort to adapt to their needs. There actually are very few attempts to socialize them within the Church, in the sense of giving them a specific point of identification with it. We have been taking care of the child side of our man-children, to the neglect of the man side. Teens are expected to show child-like fidelity, but we are reluctant to serve their legitimate needs. We just take it for granted that they are and will continue to be members; yet they may not be taking it for granted at all. A young person may intend to drop out as soon as he/she is given the freedom to decide for oneself the question of allegiance to a faith community.

It is true to say that serious attempts to identify adolescents with the Church are being made in religious education, but we have to be even more serious about these attempts. They certainly have to be more serious than our woeful high school CCD programs. We have to adapt our liturgies to the young people; we have to give them opportunities to come together precisely as adolescent members of the Church. We have been successful in our CYO sports programs of bringing them together over athletics. Now we have to try to bring them together over faith. We certainly have to involve the young themselves much more in the planning of our religious education programs.

Take the example of Joe Slattery, a young man living in Brooklyn, New York. He went to a public high school for three years before dropping out and becoming a laborer. Joe is a gifted person, with a deep sense of faith and commitment to Christ. He once told the writer what it was like struggling for faith as a teenager. Belonging to a devout Irish-Catholic family in the old Greenpoint section of Brooklyn, all Joe had to do each Sunday was go across the street to St. Cecilia's Church for Mass. But Joe preferred instead to head for the candy store. As he put it, "The Mass meant nothing to me, and so I preferred the liturgy at Sal's." He would sit and sip coffee with his friends until Mass was over, then get a report on the homily from one of the after-Mass customers before returning diligently home. It was only when he was in his early twenties that he discovered, with the help of a group of young Cursillistas, the significance of his faith.

There is an important catechetical lesson to be pondered in Joe's story. The community of St. Cecilia's on a Sunday morning meant little to Joe. While he was in the process of developing an adult faith, the Eucharist was not a good starting place, at least not for him. The Eucharist is a terminal point for faith already lived and a starting point for faith about to be lived. It is the summit of the Christian life and is so expressive of one's entire grasp of the Christian mystery. To Joe it expressed nothing but boredem, task, and magic. He had not yet achieved a point of faith that would desire expression in Eucharist. And to Joe what was expressive of much in his life was the informal gathering in Sal's candy store. Here he was able to discuss his problems and his loves: school, family, sports, girls. These concerns should have provided the real living out of which could have flowed the Eucharist. That candy store was probably a good catechetical situation, lacking only the catechist to help the teenagers see Christ at the heart of life and to lead them to celebrate that presence. Modern catechists will have to become even more diligent in recognizing and even in seeking out the varied environments that could be catechically valuable.

The Question of Content

If there is any validity to the previous three points, then renewed attention should be given the question of religious education for adolescents. In the course of the catechetical renewal, it has become increasingly clear that much of the content of religious education is already present in the people we are trying to lead to Christ. Even the smallest child already has a history of personal relationships, has already been formed to a certain extent. All people carry around with them their own personal baggage of experiences, perceptions and, above all, memories. This is the primary content of religious education, in the sense that it is what must be built upon. Focusing more realistically on the situation of those to be catechized, including the personal baggage of each, allows us actually to get back to the style of the primitive catechesis of the early Church. It is an instructive exercise to reread Peter's sermon in Acts 2:14-17, to see how careful he is to speak to the situation of his hearers. Peter's sermon content is tailored to the content of his listeners.

This question ultimately involves that of goals and priorities in religious education. With regard to a systematic presentation of historical and theoretical religious content, it is not a question of discarding it, but rather of asking the further questions: when and how. Counselors of the young realize that they are constantly grappling with the meaning of the everyday events in their lives. Young people are engaged in a process of integration, of piecing together the meaning of life. Like the Blacks of Harlem, they are intent on exploring their own inner space and prefer to disdain questions that do not seem to touch on their daily concerns. It is at this juncture that they are finally ready to understand their faith. Catechists need to allow them to explore their own questions and assist them in this exploration, setting up environments where they feel comfortable doing so.

In conclusion, it should be the supreme mark of success when teenagers can look back on a religious education program, or even one session in a program, and say that they enjoyed attending it. The young do not learn best by listening to the golden words of teachers; they learn by being on their feet and doing things, by acting out skits, by being given a chance to laugh at themselves, by being able to engage in the kind of seriousness that genuine laughter makes possible. They learn especially from people they can be comfortable with, who can laugh with them and grieve with them and pray with them, who love them enough to point out childishness when they see it. Play is a human need, a constant one, enabling people to be authentically serious and reflective.

In other words, the answer to the religious education dilemmas set in catechizing young people does not lie in technology. Neither filmstrip viewer, overhead projector, records, nor movies by the truck-load have the answer. The key is in the young themselves, in their desire to explore their own experiences, in their desire to speak of their deepest concerns with those who will listen with understanding. This kind of listening can take place individually or in groups. The focus here has been specially on the group. It has too long been ignored in religious education. Here young people can become Church—or anti-Church. Just which it is, at least in part, is our responsibility.

NOTES

1. Here "socialization" is being used in a somewhat broader sense than that used by Berger and Luckmann in *The Social Construction of Reality* (New York: Doubleday and Company, Anchor Edition, 1967), p. 138. "Socialization" in my specialized usage here refers to all those group processes by

which an individual assimilates the understandings of a group. My usage is close to what could be called "formation of community."

2. Paulo Freire has developed his program of conscientization to help peoples, especially peasant classes, become more aware of, and thus better able to shape, the social forces that have such a decisive influence on their lives. See Paulo Freire, *The Pedagogy of the Oppressed* (New York: Herder and Herder, 1970).

3. Environmental catechesis can be a useful term for pointing to the social context which is operative in all human interaction. This aspect of catechesis received much attention at the Sixth International Catechetical Study Week, at Medellin, Colombia, 1968, although the term "environmental catechesis" itself was not used. See Jacques Audinet, "Catechetical Renewal in the Contemporary Situation," *Teaching All Nations*, 5:4 (October, 1968), p. 418-434.

4. Although education itself should foster what Paulo Friere calls a "critical consciousness," i.e., a critical awareness of social structures, the focus in the present treatment will be on the need for directors of youth programs especially to become aware of these structures. Anyone who wishes to catechize modern youth must, through painstaking observation, become attuned to the "thematic universe" of the young. See, Freire, *op. cit.*, pp. 75-118.

5. John W. Gardner, *Self Renewal* (New York: Harper and Row, 1967), p. 144.

6. Edgar Z. Friedenberg, *The Vanishing Adolescent* (New York: Dell Publishing Co., Laurel Edition, 1962), pp. 29-30.

7. "In every situation the two elements [that of the Church and the culture of a particular country] are intertwined and the work of evangelization depends on the relationship of the one to the other within the given situation. The situation is never neutral: the Church and man have already met each other within a cultural context, within a history. . . . At any rate we can never start from scratch; the point-of-departure is this whole in which Christianity and the human adventure are mixed: this ensemble of words, representations, attitudes, relationships, conflicts that make up the experience of the whole human group." Audinet, *op. cit.*, 428-429.

8. Information on this program can be obtained from:

Young Life Campaign, West Monument St., Colorado Springs, Colorado 80901, U.S.A.

9. In secular education as well, aspects of learning broader than simple academic achievement are now being given much attention. See, for example, Christopher Jencks, "A Reappraisal of the Most Controversial Education Document of Our Time," New York *Times Magazine*, August 10, 1969, pp. 12-13, 34, 36, 38, 42, 44; esp. p. 44.

10. See, for example, Patrick C. Rooney, "Religious Instruction in the Context of Catholic Schooling," in Lee and Rooney (eds.), *Toward a Future for Religious Education* (Dayton, Ohio: Pflaum Press, 1970) pp. 5-29.

11. Lawrence R. Hepburn notes the research showing religion to be among the topics most discussed by high school age students. See Lawrence R. Hepburn, "Religion in the Social Studies," *Religious Education*, 66:3 (May-June, 1971), 174-175. Similarly, Allport finds that religious questions come to the forefront with the onset of puberty. See Gordon W. Allport, *The Individual and His Religion* (New York: The Macmillan Company, Macmillan Paperback Edition, 1960), p. 36.

12. Hervé Carrier, *The Sociology of Religious Belonging* (New York: Herder and Herder, 1965), p. 252.

13. *Ibid.*, pp. 247-248.

14. This point could be open to considerable misunderstanding. Certainly this is not to suggest we further extend the already extended period of adolescence in Western society. Willingness to listen and talk to young people in informal situations would lead them more naturally into the adult world and, many different age groupings.

15. Overholt reports that even college students pick the following as sources of personal assistance in religion: guidance counselors (59.7%), academic classes and related sources (45.2), friends (64.2), faculty (40.1), clergy on campus (20.2), and informal discussion groups as in a dormitory (64.2). Overholt also sees that the role of dormitory life is central in decision-making, value formation of peer groups, and crystallization of decisions. In this he finds a major ground for exploration of a new network of communications in religious work with this age group. See William A. Overholt, "College Students and Religion in an Urban University," *The Living Light*, 7:3 (Fall, 1970), pp. 31-42.

16. Unfortunately, some, forgetting one of the more deli-

cate human values, reticence, tend to equate personal discussion with psychic undressing. Also unfortunate is the tendency on the part of some to turn group dynamics into those versions of sensitivity sessions that are more accurately called "psychic peep shows." Balance will be kept if our constant goal is education for freedom and liberation, rather than for domination or manipulation. By "self-revelation" in this context is meant, especially, acknowledging and sharing the faith values that motivate one's life.

17. Obviously relaxation is not the only condition of learning. Anxiety and tension provide another and a vital impetus for learning. For a good treatment of the role of tension in learning, see Richard M. Jones, *Fantasy and Feeling in Education* (New York: Harper and Row, Colophon Edition, 1968), pp. 55-86.

18. Pierre Babin, *Crisis of Faith* (New York: Herder and Herder, 1963), pp. 86-87.

Part II

Setting Up Programs

Components of Successful Youth Catechetical Programs

Michael Warren

During a two-year period, 1973-1975, the writer surveyed at the diocesan level the situation of youth catechesis in out-of-school programs. He met with representatives of almost every diocese in the country to discuss the directions of youth catechesis in their own and neighboring dioceses. However, as a follow-up to this diocesan-level survey, he tried to identify parishes running model successful youth programs. He was curious to find out whether his own three-year experience in parish clusters in New York and Virginia was similar to the experiences of those running catechetical programs in Tucson, Spokane, and Orlando. He also wanted to find out if he could uncover components common to successful catechetical ministry to young people at the parish level.

In order to get this information, the writer asked each diocese in the United States to identify two of its best parish youth programs, and then wrote these parishes asking for a detailed description of their youth catechetical programs. The following report is a summary of the data sent in by the relatively small number of twenty-nine parishes that responded to this request for detailed information. It took weeks of pouring over the descriptions of these parish programs before being able to see the common elements hidden in the various reports. After all, the reporting parishes were geographically and demographically diverse. Some programs were based in homes, some in area centers. Some parishes used only professional teachers as catechists; others invited a cross-section of adults to engage in this ministry. Thus the first and most obvious feature of successful catechetical programs for youth in various parishes in the United States was the variety of approaches that characterized them.

More study, however, revealed another more unifying common element among these various programs. It was this: in each program there had been careful attention to relationships among all those involved in the program. Another way of expressing this commonality: every program reported was in some respect a community-centered one. There was great care given to the way people came together. Attention was paid to relationships among all in the program, among the adults, among the young people, and between the young people and the adults. Where parishes were successful at the relational level they were also successful catechetically. The following paragraphs describe in some detail the community-centered component of these parish programs, before going on to describe other features common to them: variety, planning, and informality.

I
COMMUNITY-CENTERED PROGRAMS

What do we mean by community-centered programs? To repeat, these are programs that successfully develop relationships among the adults, between the adults and young people, and among the young people. At this point I would like to examine each of these relationships in turn.

Relationships among Adults

These relationships are fostered and encouraged in many different ways.

As a Support Group. In many well-planned parish youth catechetical programs the adult catechists actually form a support group in which individual catechists find help and encouragement. In such parishes, adult catechists meet together regularly but in informal settings. Such meetings sometimes occur as de-briefing sessions after a program. Intelligent use of de-briefing can turn a weekly meeting into an in-service training program for all involved. Here the adults discuss what happened and why—in some places over beer and sandwiches. This is an atmosphere where they can share their successes and failures, knowing that even failures can be a source of learning and future growth. Under a leader who convenes this group these adults can also exchange ideas about what is happening in their program and about future directions they would like to take. Thus they become involved in the evolution of the program. Such adults work not in isolation but in co-relation.

As a Fellowship. In some parish catechetical programs, adults form a fellowship of faith. They pray regularly together. In addition to meeting to plan, they also meet to share their faith with one another. Such faith-sharing sessions take many forms: periods of prayer at the end of other types of meetings, days of recollection, retreats, celebrations of unity in the Eucharist. There is no formula for developing a faith dimension among adults. It is more a matter of attitude, especially in the coordinator or director of a catechetical program. This attitude recognizes that if adults are to assist the young in growth in faith, they too must be actively engaged in their own development. It may be that when adults find that their catechetical ministry is aiding their own development as persons they will be most inclined to continue as catechists. At a recent meeting of catechetical leaders in Atlanta a trainer of catechists shared the following insight based on her work: those adults who have developed an ability to pray together and to talk about their own faith tend also to be the most flexible and comfortable in dealing with young people in non-classroom situations. These adults are quicker to realize that classrooms are not the only or even the best places in which to help young people grow in faith. They tend to be more free in trying out other models. Thus this trainer has built into her program a prayer and faith-sharing dimension. It makes sense. As their own understanding of faith becomes centered in their personal lives and able to be expressed in personal terms instead of solely in doctrinal formulations, these catechists rely less on a highly structured catechesis.

As a Friendship Group. Although I cannot say what levels of friendship develop among catechists in good youth catechetical programs, yet from the low-key contact with one another as a support group and as a faith fellowship one would suspect that in addition to a good deal of friendliness, various degrees of friendship also emerge.

Relationships between Adults and Teens

These programs also attend to adult-teen relationships. Obviously, some of the good relationships that evolve between teens and adults come about naturally. A mature, well-balanced adult who has a sense of humor and a love of young people will easily develop a good relationship with kids. What I am referring to here is something that happens because it has been planned at the program level. By what means?

By Joint Planning. Young people help plan and run the catechetical program they themselves are in. The adults have provided for a young authentic participative role in running the program. Representatives of the young people are given a say in program development, implementation, and evaluation. Moreover, the young may serve on a variety of other working groups, dealing with publicity, service programs, and social athletic events. In short, the input of all is actively sought, recognized and appreciated. More and more parish programs for youth, and especially for older youth, are relying on the input of the young themselves.

By Creating an Atmosphere of Friendship. Some parishes have paid special attention to the atmosphere or setting for youth catechesis. The program has been organized for informal interaction between adults and the young. The program is not limited to rectangular spaces called classrooms within which from ten to thirty adolescents sit and listen to the words of a single adult. Rather, the program is designed around a variety of activities, all of which encourage the young and adults to be together in a friendly, mutually enriching way. Retreats, a rap session, field trips, and, as we shall see, a variety of approaches are used to create a relationship of friendship between the teens and adults.

In his recent book, *Five Cries of Youth,* Merton Strommen remarks that the basic or primal ministry to the young is the ministry of friendship. This fact is something skillful catechists have long known. In this connection, the choice of language by some of these parishes was interesting. Many avoided the term "teacher" to refer to their adult catechists, preferring instead to call them simply "adults" or "leaders" or "resource persons." One report described these adults as "catalyst, participant, facilitator, motivator." Such a use of language may highlight a distinctive role for the catechist dealing with youth in out-of-school programs.

What are some of the things individual adults do to foster this bond of friendship with young people? Some, recognizing that telephone conversation has a special intimacy for young people, make a point of phone contact with their kids. Others attend sports and social functions their kids are involved in. Some bring their wives or husbands to catechetical programs on occasion, so the young people will get to know other dimensions of their lives. Some adults are eager to be on retreat teams, since they recognize the close bond that can develop on a retreat weekend.

At the program level, adults are not put in the position of functioning primarily as disciplinarians. Programs are designed for flexibility, for a very low-key sort of discipline with few sanctions. Lyman Coleman-type group programs are designed to allow for much informal chatter while learning is going on. The only rule, and often an unwritten one, in such programs is that of listening when someone is speaking to be heard. That is simple politeness and ordinarily not a problem for young people. One group of parishes designed a program so that kids could miss a week without causing any difficulty to others. It was a large-group program, based on a different theme each week. The themes were not sequential, though they were announced in advance. The young were encouraged to come to the programs that appealed to them. However, the strategy among the adult leaders was to make certain that each week those who didn't come would regret having missed an exciting, rewarding evening. And so it was. I am told that enrollment grew from week to week until two groups had to be formed. This move toward greater flexibility and a more relaxed atmosphere paid off in a better relationship between the teens and adults. Such programs are not highly structured, though they are carefully organized. In general, the looser the structure, the more careful the organization and preparation needed to ensure its success.

Those parishes that give a priority to adult-teen relationships recognize that catechesis is not something a privileged group does for an underprivileged group. It is rather a joint venture in which both groups grow together through their efforts on one another's behalf. Catechesis is not a soup kitchen operation; it is not done in handouts from the haves to the have-nots; it is much more like a family dinner table where parents and children alike are nourished not only by the food but also by each other's presence.

Relationships among Teens

Successful catechetical programs for adolescents also pay attention to the relationships among the kids themselves. Again, as with interaction among the adults and between the adults and teens, there is a preoccupation with how people come together. These programs have shifted emphasis from the quantity of sessions and of participants to the quality of relationships among participants. If the priority is the quality of time spent together, emphasis is not on attendance but rather on the growth of those who do attend. That approach seems to help the attendance problem solve itself. Some of the forms this emphasis on teen relationships takes are as follows. There is a great deal of emphasis on small group discussion and on other types of *sharing* among the young people. Whereas catechesis for young people was once dominated by input, there seems to be a shift to expressivity, that is, to procedures that will encourage them to make sense out of what they have been told and to express what it means in relation to their own personal lives. Some parishes are doing youth catechesis out of a basic service model. The young people engage in service projects as an effort to express their faith in action. They come together at regular intervals to pray about, talk about, and learn more about the further dimensions of their Christian service. Input is handled exclusively in full-day retreat-type programs that are planned as they are needed.

There is also emphasis on leadership development. Young people are asked to take leadership roles in running various aspects of their own programs. I have already mentioned something about this important development. Retreats are probably the most concrete example of a valuable type of leadership development. The majority of youth retreat programs now in this country make use of teenage team members who give carefully prepared talks based on their own personal experience of the Gospel. I have heard many such talks over the past ten years and they have a unique and very moving power. Such a role in a retreat develops not only leadership but also an authentic ministry among the young themselves. What I am saying is that the best catechetical programs are now developing a catechetical ministry among the young. Their young people are becoming skilled catechists in their own right. That is why one small-town catechetical center could report that fifty percent of its adult catechists had themselves as kids gone through the center's programs.

As a result of such indirect leadership training, catechetical programs are helping teens exercise a peer ministry, a ministry to their own age group. That ministry is at root a ministry of friendship which provides basic care and concern so needed by the young. Once this dynamic of caring and service to other young people takes root among even a small group of leaders in a catechetical program the complexion of the entire program changes for the better. The program then generates its own life. It ceases to run on the feel of adult pressures and cajoling. It is energized by a communal life of its own.

II

OTHER FEATURES OF SUCCESSFUL PARISH PROGRAMS

Planning

Careful planning has been the underlying motif in the above explanation of the successful parish program. There is not one-time planning, that is, planning in September for the entire year. Planning usually is done in segments. The first sequence of events is planned, run and then evaluated before the next sequence is run. This type of planning is admittedly time-consuming. Yet it pays off, especially if the planning process involves the young people themselves.

The following are some other planning strategies being used by parish programs:

● a weekly or bi-weekly bulletin sent to the adult leaders, informing them of the precise goals and procedures of a particular week's programs;

● a regular weekly "de-briefing" session among all the adult leaders of a particular age group;

● a special planning session run over several weeks between the fall and spring sessions, during which the weekly program is shut down (inventory time); one parish schedules three planning workshops each year;

● keeping the young people informed of at least the general directions of the program, in addition to providing them with a written bulletin of events and activities.

Variety

One of the results that careful planning makes possible is a deliberate variety in programming. At any rate, most of the parishes reporting in my survey showed a good deal of variety in what they were doing for youth. The most common format in use is presentation by the catechist followed by small-group discussion. However, an assortment of active educational procedures like educational games, role playing, problem solving, guest lectures, field trips, all-day and weekend retreats, and large group celebrations are all apt to be utilized at times in the course of a program. One parish reports using "everything from panels to rap sessions, dramatic playlets and the rock opera, *Tommy*, to expand liturgies and full length films."

In addition to variety of educational procedures, parishes also report a range of other activities serving various needs of young people. Some offer one-to-one counseling for those desiring it. Others have lively social action programs, as well as regularly scheduled social activities, such as recreational trips, dances, talent shows and so forth. Social activities to which the young can invite their friends who do not participate in the catechetical program appear to be a useful means of publicity.

These then are some of the common elements found in parish catechetical programs that have been identified by diocesan catechetical staff persons as successful. It is important to keep in mind the variety of approaches that characterized these programs. Such variety suggests that a successful catechetical approach to youth cannot be neatly blueprinted from somebody else's design. What might be appropriate to a large urban parish might not be feasible for a rural area. On the other hand the interaction that characterized the programs studied suggests that good catechesis emerges from efforts at becoming a common unity joined in a common faith in Jesus and in a common love and respect for one another. Such a common unity does not just happen. It is an achievement, the result of careful effort by all involved. One might expect the results of such efforts to be their own reward.

Catholic High Schools: Organizing the Religion Department

Louis Dalton, C.F.X.

In preparing the material for this book, I felt the need to focus on ministry to youth in the context of a Catholic high school. One would suppose that with the catechetical renewal, religion programs in high schools have uniformly improved throughout the country. From informal talks with many high school religion teachers, I conclude that this improvement is spotty. Much work needs to be done. Further, models for improving the performance of a religion department need to be developed.

Thus, I asked Louis Dalton, C.F.X., to prepare an account of his efforts to organize and direct the religion department of St. Xavier High School, Louisville, Kentucky. As a friend and colleague, he took time out from his studies at Catholic University to prepare the following report, which is especially valuable for its realistic account of the hard work involved in setting up an effective religion program.   *Michael Warren*

─────────────── ▲ ───────────────

Any attempt to give a detailed blueprint for developing a high school religion program would be equivalent to taking a position that life is static, that Christianity is simply a body of knowledge to be conveyed to others, and that the task of the

93

religion teacher is simply to know the correct answers and methods of religious education. Therefore, the primary purpose of
this paper is to raise questions, to try to put questions into perspective, and, one might hope, to aid in the process of growth
and development of a religion department.

For too long religion teachers have sought the correct text
book, the latest methods, and the most relevant topics for religious education. This quest for relevance is seen as coming from
outside the religion teacher. The new is always seen as attractive
trappings for a well worn message. Today, because of the conservative backlash, the quest is sometimes seen as a return to more
stable and secure times where doctrine is supreme and questions
secondary. However, this quest for Christian meaning only bears
fruit when it comes from within. To use the words from a song
by Cat Stevens, many religious educators are "on the road to
find out." There is great enthusiasm and dedication. Yet, the answers are always sought from outside. The expert is always
called upon for the correct answers and the latest methods. However, just knowing the answers and methods is not enough.
Where this is the case, the answers will have a hollow ring and
the method will be perceived as another gimmick. In this frantic
quest the true secret of Christianity eludes the religious educator.
The answer lies within. Just as Christianity requires a personal
commitment that necessitates an integration of that message in
every fiber of being, so likewise, a religion department has to live
that process it advocates. The answer has to come from within.

This paper will attempt to give some direction to that quest
of making a religion department a living Christian structure that
will proclaim the Christian message. Here, it is important to
note a couple of words. First, direction means looking at options, seeing various approaches to the questions. It does not
mean giving the correct solution. Second, the word structure has
suffered from a bad press in the last few years. However, structure is important. Everyone needs structure and especially a
group of teachers and students in a highly specialized subject.
The question to be considered is the dynamics of the structure
because structure can facilitate growth or it can hinder growth.
There are four areas of organization that this paper will consid-

er. The first area of organization to be considered will be that of the primary questions and relationships, the second, the organization of the program, the third, the organization of the teachers, and the fourth, the organization of materials.

What does it mean when one says that the answer lies within? Basically it means that the religion department has to commit itself to that process of growth that the Christian message demands. How is that commitment reflected in a religion department? Does it flow simply from the words that one uses? No, it lives only in the structures and the interaction of the people involved in the department. A lot of ink has been spilled concerning the school becoming a faith community. So often Christianity is taken as a game of semantics. To say, "The faith community of the school will celebrate liturgy," does not, in and of itself, make it different than to say, "There will be a school mass." The words do not change the reality. Hopefully, new words and new terminology reflect a new understanding and perception of that reality.

It is the willingness of a department to explore the reality that the words reflect that enables the answers to come from within. Just as a person has to ground himself/herself in terms of fundamental questions, so likewise does a religion department. Questions such as, "Who am I?," "What is the purpose of my exsitence?," and "Where am I going?," all have to be worked out in relation to the Christian message. A person is never complete, but always called to wider horizons, always called to respond to what he or she is called to become. Christianity is a growth process in relationship with the person of Jesus. If a person believes that Christianity is a growth process that requires a personal response from within, then there are several consequences that follow from that position. First, a person is always called to greater horizons, a greater awareness of his/her relationship with God, others, and self. This process is never completed. Therefore a high school religion program is only a part of that life long process. It is not the total process. (How many times has it been said that if they don't get it in high school they will never hear it?) Second, a high school religion program is a structured process (whether those involved are conscious of the structure and its consequences or not) that is intended to convey the message and also initiate or further the process of Christian living. The structured process (the religion program) should convey or reflect the basic message and process of Christian living that is being proclaimed. In other words, if the teachers in a religion department cannot sit down and talk to one another and agree on workable solutions, then how can the department expect to proclaim what it does not even practice? If the structure, the way the department is run, the way the teachers relate to other teachers, and the way teachers interact with students, don't reflect the Christian message, then words become empty, meaningless symbols.

How does a religion department organize itself to be both a means of growth for the religion faculty and the students? Religious education is concerned with living. There are no short cuts to a happy life. It is so easy to get tied up in method and forget what one is about. It is so easy to want to please everyone immediately and forget about long range goals and purposes. It is so easy to put one's faith in new programs, new text books, new media, and forget that religious education is involved with people and that people are the most important product. It is so easy to be concerned with the fluff of reality in which everyone is fascinated though not fulfilled, than to deal with the nitty-gritty of reality that calls for understanding, compassion and love. How does a department avoid these pitfalls? The department has to discard the cardboard caricature of itself and commit itself to exploring the fundamental questions of purpose and meaning. This is not a commitment that happens at a two hour department meeting and then is forgotten. It is a life-long commitment for the religion teacher. A department is never finished or complete. There are no perfect or ideal programs. The department and the program, one would hope, is always in the process of becoming.

Organizing the Question

A religion department is faced with a multitude of questions and problems and is often expected to produce immediate an-

FUNDAMENTAL RELATIONSHIPS

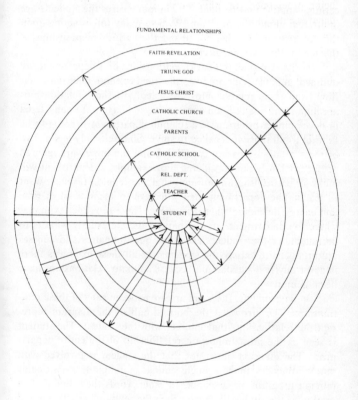

FUNDAMENTAL RELATIONSHIPS

FAITH-REVELATION

TRIUNE GOD

JESUS CHRIST

CATHOLIC CHURCH

PARENTS

CATHOLIC SCHOOL

REL. DEPT.

TEACHER

STUDENT

Diagram One

swers. There are so many groups giving advice to the department that it becomes difficult to know where to begin. The parents of the students are asking for one thing, the principal wants a program that will please everyone, the teachers all have ideas concerning what should be done, and in many cases the students are indifferent about any program. With so many forces acting upon the department, it is helpful to put the various relationships of the department into perspective.

In diagram one, the basic relationships of a department are outlined and in diagram two, the fundamental questions that flow from these relationships are listed. All these relationships are important to a religion department and have to be considered in developing a program, if a religion department is going to be faithful to all those it is called to serve. So often, only one or two of these relationships are considered and the others are ignored or unconsciously not considered. For example, a department will build an entire program around what the religion teachers want to teach. The department then will have to spend a lot of time and energy defending what it is doing. There are other examples where the department lets the parents dictate exactly what is to be taught, or the students are given questionnaires and courses are produced to satisfy the students. In all these examples there is never any real satisfaction because so many relationships have been ignored.

In diagram one, there are arrows between each of these relationships. The arrows at the bottom half of the diagram represent the relationships that interact with the student. The student is seen as the most important relationship of the entire department. The diagram illustrates that the student is involved with more influences than a single course in religion, a particular religion program, or a school. In other words the religious formation of the student is greater than the religion department and the school. Religion departments at times in their zeal for conversion forget that the department plays only a part in the entire religious formation of the student. It would be well that the parents of the students be made aware of this limited role of the department and possibly the high expectations placed on a department would become more realistic.

FUNDAMENTAL QUESTIONS

WHAT IS FAITH?

WHAT IS REVELATION? HOW DOES IT HAPPEN?

WHO IS GOD?

WHAT DOES THE MYSTERY OF THE TRINITY
MEAN IN THE LIFE OF THE CHRISTIAN?

WHO IS JESUS CHRIST?

WHAT IS THE GOOD NEWS?

WHAT IS THE NATURE AND PURPOSE OF THE
CATHOLIC CHURCH?

WHAT IS THE ROLE OF PARENTS IN RELIGIOUS
EDUCATION?

WHAT IS THE PURPOSE OF A CATHOLIC
SCHOOL?

WHAT IS THE ROLE OF THE RELIGION
DEPARTMENT IN A CATHOLIC SCHOOL?

WHAT IS THE ROLE OF THE RELIGION
TEACHER?

HOW IS THE GOSPEL MESSAGE PROCLAIMED TO
PROTECT THE RIGHTS AND FREEDOM OF EACH
STUDENT?

- -

FORMULATION OF PRINCIPLES OF THE
RELIGION DEPARTMENT

FORMULATION OF GENERAL GOALS OF
THE RELIGION DEPARTMENT

Diagram Two

The top half of diagram one illustrates the communication that has to occur between each of these relationships. The understanding of each of these realities should be consistent with the department's understanding of each of the other realities. In the diagram, each of these realities are placed in concentric circles. By illustration, each reality fits into the next circle. The interdependence of each of these realities can be better visualized if one were to remove from the diagram any circle not found to be truly consistent and harmoniously related with the others. They are meant to be in a harmonious unity with each other; otherwise they clash badly. For example, a department's understanding of faith gives meaning to the department's understanding of revelation. Likewise, a department's understanding of revelation reflects on the department's understanding of faith. Continuing through the circle, the department's understanding of faith and revelation gives direction to the department's understanding of God and so forth through each of the relationships.

It would be a mistake to give the impression that the mysteries of the Christian faith can be so easily categorized. The diagram is intended to show the interdependence of these realities. One could expect that from a department's commitment to growth, the complexities of these realities will be seen more in depth, year after year, as the department works on understanding itself and its purpose.

How does a department begin to deal with the multiplicity of relationships with which it is involved? Who makes the decisions concerning what the department should be about? Does the department set up a committee that is representative of each of these relationships and then produce a program? No, a committee would only produce a fragmented program that would please no one. The comment of the wag who observed that a camel is a horse produced by a committee seems very appropriate here. What then are some guidelines for orchestrating these relationships that affect a religion program? I offer seven areas that must be attended to if these relationships are to function properly.

First, before any of the relationships are considered, the

members of the religion department have to be willing and free enough to sit down and discuss the purpose of the department together. This willingness of the teachers requires a commitment to ongoing solutions rather than absolute answers. This is where an understanding of Christianity as a growth process is important. If the teachers are able to discuss and share with one another, then an examination of the fundamental questions and relationships is possible. This ability for teachers to work together doesn't just happen. It requires knowledge of communication skills that have to be practiced over a period of time. A religion department has to have basic communication skills in order that a discussion of the fundamental questions and relationships can be considered.

Second, the religion faculty working together have to take an honest look at its students. This involves more than just giving out a questionnaire and asking students what courses of studies are desired. If students knew everything that they wanted to learn about religion, then there would be no reason for the students to be in a religion class. Religious education is more an awareness of the questions of life rather than knowing the answers to specific problems. This does not mean that students should not be consulted. More important than questionnaires is the teachers' awareness of who their students are. This means that the teachers are able to have empathy with their students. The problems and joys of a teenager are best seen through the eyes of a teenager. Teachers can learn more about the needs and expectations of students by talking with students than through a questionnaire. Basically, such understanding demands a commitment to communication and understanding of the students. Programs should be designed for students with a knowledge of the students.

Knowledge and awareness of the psychology of the adolescent is important in designing a religion program. It is here, looking at real students, that critical questions for the department have to be answered. It is very easy to talk about faith commitment, knowledge of the Bible, and reception of the sacraments, in terms of ideals or goals. However, it is only when these goals have been sifted through the world of the teenager, can they become realistic and tangible goals. By "sifted through the world of the teenager" is meant that the needs, the emotional, and intellectual maturity of the teenager have been considered. For example, all would agree that knowledge and use of the Scriptures is a basic source of growth for the Christian. However, to conclude that freshmen in high school should study a year of scripture in order to give them a foundation for their Christian faith does not necessarily follow from the above conclusion. When most freshmen in high school are learning how to write a paragraph and read a short story in their English class, it does not make sense to teach freshmen the literary genres of the Bible in religion class. I am not saying that scripture cannot be used with freshmen students. What I am saying is that an exegesis of the Bible is not appropriate for freshmen.

Third, the religion department has to be aware of the school's stance towards Christian education. A starting point for looking at the school is an examination of the school's philosophy. More important than what is stated on paper is a determination of how that philosophy is carried out in the day to day life of the school. A religion department has to realize that it is only one department in the school and that all the departments are involved in living out that philosophy. Many times a religion department sees itself as an agent for change within the school. This is a very legitimate and important function of the department. However, if the department places itself in opposition to the rest of the school, then the department becomes a source of disagreement, anger, and frustration, rather than a source of growth. Therefore, a religion department has to maintain a balance in being an agent of change and growth without becoming an agent of antagonism, mistrust and alienation.

Fourth, the religion department has to consider the parents of the students in developing a program. Probably this relationship has been, and still is, the most neglected relationship of all with which a department deals. Parents have a right to know what their children are being taught. Parents should know more about the religion program than is contained in a vague course description. Parents should have a detailed description of the philosophy, the goals, and objectives of the religion department. The department is responsible for answering the questions of the parents. Sound, fundamental reasons should be offered to the parents for the way the program is run and for the content of the program. A program may be working well, but if the department cannot communicate with the parents as to the rationale for the program, problems are certain to arise. Again, awareness and skill in communication is important here. Therefore, a religion department should have an ongoing dialogue with parents in developing and in running a program. The main responsibility for communication lies with the school and the religion department and not with the parents.

Fifth, a religion department has to be aware of how it presents the church and also be aware of the various documents that the church has issued on Christian education and religious education. Department members should study these documents and as a group draw the implications that these documents have for their own situation. It is from the study of these documents that the general goals and objectives of a department should emerge. Key materials such as the *Documents of Vatican II, To Teach as Jesus Did*, the *General Catechetical Directory* and the *National Catechetical Directory* give an understanding of the fundamental relationships and the fundamental questions facing a religion department. Here the task of the department is to integrate the principles and guidelines of these documents into a living program. However, awareness of the relationships and the implications of the principles and guidelines is the first step before a program can begin.

Also, a religion department has to be aware of how it presents the church or rather how the religion program reflects the church. For example, it would be well for the members of the department to study Avery Dulles' *Models of The Church* (Garden City: Doubleday and Company, 1974) and then determine the model(s) of the church that the program presents or should be presenting. Also, the study of the documents listed above will aid the process of determining how the church is presented and the consequences of that presentation.

Sixth, the religion department has to examine its own understanding of the person of Jesus, the Trinity, the nature of revelation and the nature of faith. Why is this important? If a department sees faith as a commitment and assent to a body of knowledge or revealed truths, then the department will have a different understanding of what a religion program is about than a department which sees faith as an attitude that determines one's view of reality and calls one to wider horizons in perceiving that reality. A department which sees God as an outside God, an over-and-against God, will have a different understanding of what a religion program is about than a department which sees God as immanent and transcendent. A department that starts with a descending Christology will have a different emphasis than a department that begins with an ascending Christology.

In summary, there has to be an acknowledgement that there is development and also a plurality of understanding within theology today. To ignore this reality does not make it go away. A religion faculty has to be willing to discuss their own understanding of these realities and the implications that the understanding has for a religion program. Because there are no easy solutions to these questions, a department has to commit itself to a growth process of dealing with the mysteries of the faith.

Seventh, a religion department has to be willing to involve itself with all these relationships in a dynamic process. The main ingredient of this process is communication. Where there is an attitude of growth and understanding, as opposed to dogmatic answers, then this process will produce healthy, imaginative, and stimulating programs.

Here, it is important to note that what is being advocated cannot be accomplished in one or two meetings of the department. Anytime there is an attempt at communication there will necessarily be misunderstanding. Therefore, the department has to be open to communication at all times. It is through dialogue that the department will grow and also develop worthwhile programs. It is this attitude of growth that is needed rather than an attitude of producing the perfect program. It is a recognition that the program is for people and the program will grow and develop to the degree that the people involved are committed to growth.

Organizing the Program

Once a religion department has examined the fundamental relationships and questions, then the task of putting together a program can become a reality. From the consideration of the fundamental questions and relationships should flow an understanding of the goals and objectives of a high school religion program. This should not be seen simply as a linear process. That is, when the fundamental questions and relationships have been considered then that process is over. It is necessary for the religion department to return from time to time to these fundamental questions in order to gain greater understanding and depth of the purpose and goals of the department. To translate the objectives and goals of the department into a specific program is the next challenge of the department.

How are the general goals and objectives of the department put into action? How do these abstract goals become real and form the backbone of a program? For example, the document *To Teach as Jesus Did*, lists message, community, and service as the threefold goal of a Catholic school. This particular document does not list any ways of making these goals a reality. However, mere talking about these goals and their desirability does not make them a reality. Message, community, and service are reflected in the actions and the structures within the school. For the religion department these goals are reflected in the programs of the department which includes the specific goals, the content, the method, and the materials of each of these programs.

For a school to say that message, community, and service are "taken care of" by the fact the school has liturgies within the school, classes in which religion is taught, and a service program, is to miss the point of *To Teach as Jesus Did*. These realities are never achieved but are always in the process of becoming. The reality of community is brought about by the commitment to the process of developing community, not from finding specific programs that prove that one has community. When a department or an entire school has to prove that it is Christian or Catholic then the essence of the Christian message is being distorted. The commitment to live and proclaim the message makes that message a reality. The commitment to be of service within the school community, and to the larger community, makes service a reality. Service is not proven through a service program or through a Thanksgiving food drive.

This commitment to being and becoming community, to being and growing in the message and to being and becoming of service is not an abstract commitment. This commitment has to be translated into specific goals and objectives that are reflected in particular programs, methods, content and materials. Again, it should be noted that these goals are always pursued, never conquered.

In developing specific goals, the documents listed before should be used as the primary sources. In articulating specific goals, the types of programs that the department will be involved in should be differentiated. For the sake of convenience I will list three separate programs for discussion. The three headings of classroom program, retreat program, and service program could cover all the activities in which a high school department is engaged.

I have deliberately not made the liturgical activities of the school a separate program for two reasons. First, the liturgical activities should flow from the classroom program. Second, school liturgies should not be seen as the sole responsibility of the religion department, but the responsibility of the entire school. When the entire school is responsible for the liturgical life of the school, then the false dichotomy that all activities that are religious have to be sponsored and run by the religion department is broken down.

Below in outline form I have listed an approach to developing the specific goals for each program.

Stage One: Development of The Purpose of The Religion Department

How: Consideration of Fundamental Relationships and Questions

Results: A. Principles of Religious Education
          B. General Goals of the Religion Deparrment

Stage Two: Development of Specific Goals and Objectives for the Religion Programs

How: Consideration of the principles and General Goals of Religious Education

Results: A. General Goals for Classroom Program
          1. General Objectives for Freshmen Program
          2. General Objectives for Sophomore Program
          3. General Objectives for Junior Program
          4. General Objectives for Senior Program

          B. General Goals for Retreat Program
          1. General Objectives for Freshmen Program
          2. General Objectives for Sophomore Program
          3. General Objectives for Junior Program
          4. General Objectives for Senior Program

          C. General Goals for Service Program
          1. General Objectives for Freshmen Program
          2. General Objectives for Sophomore Program
          3. General Objectives for Junior Program
          4. General Objectives for Senior Program

After looking at the above outline, a person can conclude that all that is being asked is that the goals and objectives of a program be listed. This is correct. However, the important part of the process is *the process itself*. A department can find published many outlines of goals and objectives for high school religion programs. It is the willingness of the department to immerse itself in formulating these goals and objectives that gives the program life and vitality. Obviously, published programs can be used for guidelines and directions, but the department has to develop a program of its own that flows from the conviction of the department.

Here, a word of caution should be made concerning the development of goal statements. Goal statements are not ends in themselves. They are only means to an end. The program is for people, and the teachers and the students always have to be kept in mind. What does this consideration mean in terms of developing goal statements? It means that the interdependence of all the relationships has to be kept in mind if goal statements are not to become the new absolutes. The goal statements have to be tested, modified and clarified by the teachers and the students. The uniqueness of each teacher and of each student will bring a new understanding to the scope and dimensions of the goal. Growth will occur in a department where this process is not only tolerated but actively pursued by a structured process of communication.

The above process demands time and attention but it results in a stable program, whereas a program put together by a mere collecting of various materials and methods has no solid foundation. There is no cogent, well-understood rationale for the program. When parents ask for reasons for the particular content or method of the program, it is only then that the department begins to grapple with its own purpose and objectives. Even worse, a program with a weak theoretical base is susceptible to every new fad in religious education. Teachers grasp for anything that will give purpose and meaning to what is being done.

To give the impression that determining the goals and objectives is an easy task would be a mistake. This requires long hours of discussion, reflection, and reading. However, this is not an exercise simply to produce goal statements. When a department is willing to engage in questions of purpose and meaning, then the process itself will produce a new awareness of what it means to teach religion to high school students. Hopefully, it will be seen as a process that will help the teacher grow in becoming a better teacher year after year.

Organization of the Religion Teachers

My remarks throughout this paper have been addressed to a department of teachers that is recognized as a department within the school and has a chairperson to direct and guide the department. In some Catholic high schools there are only one or two teachers involved with the full-time teaching of religion while the rest of the religion faculty is drawn from other departments. Such a situation tends to give a semi-legitimate quality to the religion department. Communication becomes difficult, not because of the lack of good will, but because of the divided time and energy of the teachers involved. Communication is of the essence if the program is to be more than a collection of text books and vague course descriptions.

The content of this communication within a department would be seen in terms of the following areas. First, there has to be a willingness to share successes and failures of the various programs in which the teachers are engaged. Honest evaluation is necessary. When teachers are free enough to talk about what really goes on in their classrooms then teachers can become invaluable resources for one another. However, if the attitude prevails that one has to have the correct answer for everything, then little communication occurs. Many times failures and frustrations are disguised in terms of discontent with a text book, the need for a new course, or a need for an entire new program. When teachers cannot admit failure and successes the department is caught in the process of always having to begin anew, since very little is learned from the successes and failures of past programs. Anyone who has taught religion for the last ten years can probably remember numerous attempts at new programs. This generally occurs in the spring of the year when the frustrations of the teachers are at their highest. In sharing successes and failures foundations for building new programs can be best begun.

Second, a department has to be willing to work as a unit or as a team. Religion teachers are highly susceptible to the Messiah complex. A teacher can mistakenly come to expect a perfect, committed Christian produced by the end of the semester. The teacher expects that a complete presentation of the Christian message will produce one-hundred percent metanoia.

A high school religion program for all its dimensions has to be seen as a single program. The teachers involved in the various aspects, whether it be the classroom, retreat, or service program, all contribute to the unity of the overall program. No one teacher can do everything. A student does not have to be exposed to the concepts of the sacraments, sin, redemption, each year. This calls for an ordered, sequential program that builds on the experience and knowledge of the students from year to year. If there is no unified program, then teachers will see little reason to share their insights with one another. Instead, a hoarding mentality can develop, in which a teacher creates his/her own tight little empire.

Teamwork can avoid more serious problems, such as caused by the occasional teacher who uses religion classes for working out personal difficulties. Sometimes a teacher having difficulty with sexuality will tend to turn every class into a discussion about sex. Or a teacher having difficulty with authority can betray a preoccupation the shortcomings of the way authority is exercised in the Catholic Church. When there is no unified program and when teachers do not see themselves as part of a united effort, then all types of excesses are possible in the classroom. What is being said here is that the living out of the goals of community, message, and service, has to begin with the department itself.

Third, there has to be a willingness to experiment. Here, the word experiment is used in its true meaning of introducing a particular initiative with the knowledge that it is an experiment and that an evaluation will have to occur at the end to see if it will remain part of the overall program. Basically experiment is a commitment to evaluation and developing tools for evaluation. Many times programs are called experiments and somehow manage to become part of the overall program without any reasons being given for this incorporation. Teachers have to be willing to try new methods, new courses, and be able to evaluate them honestly and drop those which are not useful, while incorporating those which are worthwhile into the program. This evaluation is always in light of the specific goals and objectives of the program.

Fourth, a department has to be willing to plant and let grow. An example of where a department has to plant and let grow is in the development of communication skills. Many methods in religious education call for the use of discussion groups. Whether the discussion group is a group project, discussion of a reading, or a brainstorming session, it calls for the knowledge of certain communication skills. A department cannot assume that students know how to work in a discussion group. This is a skill that has to be taught. These skills can be introduced in the freshmen year and then built upon year after year. This is an example of how a unified program can contribute to the growth and development of the students year to year. Other developmental tasks such as self knowledge, clarification of beliefs and values, articulation of beliefs and values, and growth in autonomy also have to be nourished year after year. They are like threads that run through an entire program, and are not simply topics for a quarter course.

Organization of Materials

A discussion of materials for a religion program will necessarily involve a discussion of content and method. There has been a lot of discussion over content versus process, and today there is a lot of talk about returning to doctrine. Many of these arguments blur the distinction between content and method. Any topic used in classroom has a content, and generally several methods can be employed to convey the content. The materials used generally evolve from the method chosen to convey the content. What is important is that the distinction among content, method, and materials be made and also the interdependence be realized.

As far as the call for return to doctrine is concerned, it seems that in many cases it is a call for a return to a particular method, that being indoctrination. The process of indoctrination necessitates a content that does not allow for personal questioning and does not require a variety of materials. However, to believe that a high school religion program can return to a time where belief statements are pre-packaged, handed out, and then regurgitated by the students is to court disaster.

What is important is that the goals of the program be used as the guiding factor in determining content, method, and materials. Also important is to realize that through experience, that is in using specific methods and materials, in working toward specific goals, that these goals will be refined and clarified for the department.

What can be said about method, content, and materials? I strongly believe that all three have to flow from the goals and objectives of the religion program. Because this paper has not addressed itself to any specific goals or objectives for a religion program, a discussion of specific content, method, and materials is not possible. Again, to the point of overemphasis, it is through the commitment of the department to growth in understanding its purpose and meaning that a particular program is developed.

The impression should not be given that there is not a lot to learn and study in regards to content, method and materials. Just as the department has to commit itself to the study and development of goals and objectives, so likewise, a department has to devote time and energy to the study of the nature and the function of content, method and materials. Today there are many resources available for the study of content, various teaching methods and materials for religion. The key is in organizing these materials so that there is a unified purpose and meaning for the entire program.

Conclusion: Growth of the Religion Department

In diagram three, I have outlined the process for growth of a religion department. Departments that engage in this process will probably produce different programs. The process itself allows for the uniqueness and creativity of all those involved in

GROWTH OF A RELIGION DEPARTMENT

Religion Department	Knowledge and Commitment to	Fundamental Relationships
(Religion Faculty and Chairperson) ⟷	the Use and ⟷ Development of Communication Skills	⟷ Fundamental Questions
(1)	(2)	(3)

- -

Basic Principles of Rel. Ed.	General Objectives of Classroom Program
General Goals ⟷ of Rel. Ed.	General Objectives ⟶ of Retreat Program
	General Objectives of Service Program
(4)	(5)

- -

Willingness to
Experiment

Willingness to
Share Successes
and Failures

Classroom Program:
Content, Method &
Materials

Retreat Program:
Willingness to Plant ⟷ Content, Method & ⟷ Growth of a
and Let Grow   Materials   Religion Dept.

Willingness to Work   Service Program:
as a Team   Content, Method &
                        Materials

(6)   (7)

Diagram Three

the process. In an age where there is a new awareness of the individual, institutions have to be willing to adapt their structures and attitudes to this new awareness.

In looking at diagram three, the one factor that seems almost overwhelming is the time that this process requires. Time is the most important thing that one person has to share with another. If schools are going to take the goal of community seriously, then a necessary consequence is the acknowledgment that time is necessary for that process of building community. A school may have to look at its priorities and clarify them in terms of time alloted for various activities. To suppose that a department can engage in this process by having five minute meetings after school at various times throughout the semester is ludicrous.

A department should consider each of the seven areas listed in the diagram. A realistic period of time should be allowed for the necessary discussion and formulation. Resource materials that will clarify and inform in each of these areas should be available for the faculty. Full day programs where resource people are brought in to discuss a particular area should be part of the process. Programs where teachers would work on the formulation of goals, objectives, content, etc., would also be included.

Obviously, the entire process would take several years to complete judging from the amount of time most departments have for meetings during a school year. However, this should not be a cause for alarm. If growth is to occur, it takes time for that process to produce a mature, healthy program. It should be noted that growth generally involves pain. The willingness to struggle with the growth process is what gives the program its strength and vitality. To acknowledge the dynamics of growth is to realize that the program is not an entity in itself, but only the framework by which people interact with one another.

The answer comes from within. A department has to come to the realization that relationships call for an interdependence that recognizes the individual and yet provides a structure whereby the individual can find purpose and meaning. To the degree that a department pursues the answer from within that dynamic interdependence, then growth will occur.

Principles and Procedures in Youth Ministry

Richard Costello
Michael Warren

Those who have worked with young people in developing programs for and with them will recognize much sound practicality in the following article. Readers will also see in this piece many of the same principles found in all the preceding articles, but expressed in a particularly practical and concrete manner.

───────────── ▲ ─────────────

How do we lead contemporary teens into the circle of the faith community? How do we lead them to share our cherished values of Church, prayer, and the loving Father revealed in the person of Jesus? I believe there are two important ingredients for carrying on a successful ministry to young people. The first has to do with the competence and attitude of the minister and the second with the methodology he or she employs. In the first part of the following reflections I will propose some attitudes needed by those ministering to the development of teens, and in Part II I will offer some positive suggestions for designing programs for adolescents.

I

Youth Minister Attitude #1: *Be Ready To Hand Over Your Faith*

The most important thing we as adults have to offer to the young is not our expertise at giving multi-media presentations or our skill in using a text effectively. It is our faith. If we do not believe that revelation has taken place in our lives and that we have responded to it through faith, then everything else we do is simply an exercise in technique. Still more, believing that God has touched our lives and transformed us is not enough; we must be willing to try to articulate that experience.

Actually, this is the task which in the earliest days of the Church was done by the mystagogue. The mystagogue had a privileged role of instructing others in the secrets of the Christian mystery but also of leading them in a very personal way into the mystery which is in them. Jesus himself is the mystagogue before all others, the exemplar, because he shares with us the holy mystery which he himself experienced and which now he wants to evoke in us. As Donald Gray put it recently,

> "Jesus' ministry is a grace in our midst but it also summons to a task. Jesus has enacted on our behalf the essential meaning of man's relationship to the holy mystery that is God but it must be re-enacted by us on our own behalf and in our own way for it to become salvation. The mystery of destiny and freedom which I have already pointed towards in Jesus reappears, not surprisingly, in the journey of the self."

We no longer have to be sources of infinite knowledge. We must no longer feel that we have to answer all the questions. (That is not to say, however, that information is not an important segment of religious education and ministry, but rather that it is put in its proper context.) But if we do believe that revelation has occurred in our lives and that we have tried to respond in faith, then we also know that we have responded to a mystery. We have been touched by the person of Christ and in turn have reached out and touched him, but that reciprocal action has not solved all our problems or answered all our questions. But we know, and must help the young to see, that Christ is at the heart of the Christian mystery. He does not solve problems or answer questions, but simply says that it's all right not to understand completely, it's all right not to have all the answers, it's all right to be uncertain about the future and our place in it.

Youth Minister Attitude #2: *Be Ready To Hand Over True Responsibility to the Teens*

As persons involved significantly with youth, we must be prepared to give real responsibility to the teens with whom we work. Theologically, all of us would agree that adolescents are in every sense of the word full members of the church. But the reality experienced by the young is often quite different. Parish Councils are set up with little or no representation from teenagers. Folk Masses are organized and often run without adolescent involvement or with involvement limited to playing the guitar. As one young person put it to me recently, "I wonder if the church really takes us seriously; many times I feel that I am only being offered token gestures in an effort to ensure that I continue to go to Mass or if I stop, that I come back. I'm always looking for the gimmick."

Yet all of us would probably agree that the lessons of life that we have learned best were the ones which cost us the most, because we felt personally responsible for a particular project. We adults, then, must offer young people opportunities to experience failure or success in something that is important.

Let me give an example. A few years ago, when I was a member of a catechetical team working with the young people of eight parishes in Flushing, N.Y., we spent almost four months listening to their views and complaints about the church. They had little or no real concept of what the church is supposed to be, but they were very expert at zeroing in on the weak points of what it is. We decided that the best solution would be to give these young people a chance to learn what the church is all about through an experience that would involve real responsibility.

So we went to the pastors of the eight parishes and asked them if they would be willing to let the young people try to establish a separate autonomous ninth parish composed of and run by the young people themselves. Much to our delight, the pastors agreed. And so we chose a core of about forty of the most critical young people to initiate this project.

We began with a study phase, giving them books and articles to read on the nature of church and conducting sharing and discussion sessions. Then we offered them an opportunity to go away for a Youth Parish weekend, at which they were asked to tackle such questions as membership, organization, services, finances, priest, place.

It would take too much space to explain the eventual outcome of the project. It did not continue, but mainly because many of the pastors and parish councils felt threatened by the real possibility that it might be successful. But discouraging as this outcome may sound, the project was a real learning experience for the young people involved.

We have to admit that in most parishes youngsters are not taken seriously or given a real say. Merton Strommen's research found in *A Study of Generations* points to the sense of alienation and powerlessness found among young Lutherans. The same could be said of our own young people. Actually they are ready to have a say and to exercise true leadership. Of course they need guidance, but they also need a chance. The need for a chance at leadership is highlighted in the recent report, *The Education of Adolescents*, by the National Panel on High School and Adolescent Education. If this need for greater opportunities is needed in secular education, then surely it is also needed if our young are ever to feel themselves truly members of the beloved community.

I strongly believe, however, that it is most important that adults always be involved both in catechetical and recreational programs for young people. The question is, how should the adults be involved? Too often we set up our programs first and then try to find the personnel to make them go. But, as anyone knows who has set up a teacher-training program for adults who will work with adolescents, many of them feel very uncertain about their ability to handle such work.

Youth Minister Attitude #3: *Be Ready to Adapt Programs to the Gifts of Your Adult Leaders*

Programs must be established in such a manner that the adults concerned will be able to act and relate to the young people as the adult person each is. We must be careful, for instance, not to structure programs in such a narrow way as to discourage adults who would like to become involved with young people but are afraid of working in a highly structured classroom situation.

In connection with this topic, it is important to realize that those of us who are in charge of training adults to work with the young need not accept all who apply. I know how difficult it is to resist the temptation to accept anyone who volunteers, since it is so difficult to get adults interested in such work. All the same, if we strongly believe that some adult will not be effective in dealing with the young, then we have an obligation to that person, as well as to those he or she would be working with, to say "No." Three questions suggest themselves as criteria: (1) Do they see religion as a way of life or as a set of rules and commands? (2) Do they need young people more than the young people need them? (3) Are they comfortable with themselves?

Youth Minister Attitude #4: *Be Ready To Continue Your Own Way as a Pilgrim*

Young people need to realize that we too are struggling and trying to grow in faith. All of us have surely had some teenager say to us, "You keep talking about Jesus as an example. You tell us that we should imitate him. But we can't really, can we? After all, he was also God. He didn't sin. He didn't know what it was like to be tempted—I mean *really tempted*."

I think that we pose at least an analogous problem to young people by the attitude and stance that many of us take towards them. Are we willing to admit to them that we are not perfectly formed adults and Christians? Do we project the image of having arrived? That we have achieved the plateau in life called Adulthood? I believe that it is extremely important for us to show young people by words and action and attitude that we too are in process, that we too are trying to become more mature—in faith and in other ways as well. To do otherwise is to place ourselves outside their experience.

Isn't it the experience of each of us who work with young people that they force us, in a sense, to become more consciously pilgrims and to take our own journey seriously. So in a way, they have ministered to us, through their questions, their doubts, their insights, and through their own efforts to grow closer to the Lord. Which of us hasn't grown through their witness?

II

In the light of these above attitudes of persons ministering to youth, I wish to outline some suggestions for planning that affect our methodology.

1. Plan Short Rather than Long

Programs should be designed to last for a limited period of time, and overall goals for the entire program should be established as well as for each session. It is difficult to keep young people interested in a program that lasts for a whole year—as P. T. Barnum said, "Always leave 'em wanting more." Six weeks seems to be a good length, followed by an evaluation. If the group think the program has been worthwhile, then ask them if they would like to continue with another six-week one.

About goals, I think it is important that each program should be designed to lead to a particular, specific conclusion. For example, if you conduct a program with a vague goal such as "providing better liturgical experiences in the parish," you may find that what you have actually accomplished by it is to make the young people feel more relaxed with one another and with you. This might force you to be more realistic, and to consider what programs would be necessary pre-requisites for a future liturgical program.

2. *Plan Simple Rather Than Complex*

It is impossible to convey all our theological insights in one sitting. *Programs or presentations should be designed to make only one or two points, with plenty of examples.* Alka Seltzer has made a fortune on people who overindulge in eating and drinking. Whenever we overindulge, we suffer. The same is true in catechetics except that when we overindulge in programming or presenting material, it is those with whom we are working who suffer—not us. Consider the pattern of Catholic school education: all doctrine and church history in grades 1-8; all doctrine and church history in grades 9-12; all doctrine and church history in four years of college. And CCD programs try to do the same thing with less time and motivation.

One of the problems plaguing catechesis in formal school settings is the insufferable repetition of curriculum. Some schools offer all doctrine and church history in grades 1-8; all doctrine and church history in grades 9-12; all doctrine and church history in four years of college. This is clearly a mistake. Let not those ministering to youth outside of schools make the same mistake. We have an opportunity of being much more realistic and creative in communicating new understandings to young people.

3. *Plan Inclusive Rather Than Exclusive*

In conducting any program, involve the participants as far as possible in the planning and the implementation, and always involve them in the evaluation. We would think it extremely odd if someone were to suggest to us that we were hungry, then prepared the food, fed it to us, and then told us how much we enjoyed it. Yet this is what we tend to do in religious education. By involving the participants in the whole process we are telling them that they are the most important part of the program. And, especially with regard to the evaluation, by sitting down and talking with them we are admitting that we don't have all the answers and that we can learn from them, and we are increasing the grass-roots level of support for the next program.

4. *Plan for Their Needs, Not Yours*

Our starting point in programming must be where we find the young people, and we must challenge them to grow in their faith from this point. One of the biggest mistakes I have found myself making over the past two years is to give answers to questions that the young people haven't even formulated. But when we discover what questions they really are asking, then we can help them see where they really are and challenge them to grow. At times that challenge must take the form of a personal invitation from the adult: "How do you pray?" "Would you like to go for a hamburger?"

5. *Plan for Atmosphere and for Further Planning*

Atmosphere and careful planning are both extremely important. The idea of creating a coffee house type of atmosphere is good, but the place can't be the boiler-room of the school. And how many programs that were well conceived have been total flops because of minor difficulties—the bulb burned out on the projector in the middle of the movie, the record player that didn't have a long enough extension cord. The attention of the young is so limited and so tenuous that you need all the breaks you can get to hold their attention. Proper planning and care in choosing the environment will not insure success, but it will at least give you a fighting chance.

6. *Plan To Waste Time on the Teens*

We need to be *willing to spend time* with the young people with whom we are trying to work. Dealing with the adolescent is a full-time job. If you expect them to be there when you run a program, then they expect you to be there when they have something to talk about.

Adolescents need lots of time to feel comfortable with you and with one another. At times it is simply enough to be present to one another. An example of what I mean comes to mind. Recently, my uncle, who is deaf, was in the hospital. He has practically given up trying to communicate with people because of his hearing problem. Each day a 9 year old girl would come to my uncle's bed and offer him some candy, give him a picture she had drawn or show him a present she had received. No words were ever said between the two and yet much was spoken. We in religious education must also learn to speak as much by our presence as by our words.

7. *Plan To Expect and then To Accept Failures*

My experience has been that for every "successful" program that I have run there have been at least two or three total flops. Perhaps the greatest failure we experience is that no one comes to our programs, or that the half that do come the first week don't show the next time around.

All of our programs will be flops if we allow ourselves to get into the numbers syndrome. "We had 40 young people at to-night's program. It must have been a great program." Statements like this are spoken all the time, and they are not necessarily true. In fact, many times large numbers militate against effective programming. Each one who comes should feel that he/she has had an opportunity to be heard, a chance to participate and that his/her presence was noticed.

It is instructive for ministers to youth to go through the New Testament on occasion and see the patience of Jesus with his disciples. In one sense he seems to have picked a group of complete losers. But then note the patience he shows. He knows that the fruit of his work with his disciples will appear only very slowly and gradually. In so many other aspects of his own life, Jesus shows the attitude we must have: of waiting for the time of fullness to come, of waiting until God's hand will bring good out of our efforts. Remembering "God's own good time" might be a helpful corrective to our passion for measurable objectives.

8. *Plan To Learn by Doing*

Learn to trust in your own creativity. Often it is so easy to simply show a filmstrip or slavishly follow a text. All of us have a tremendous amount of untapped creativity—creativity that could be employed in program planning. The most effective medium in religious education is the medium of the person. Each of us, young and old, has a wealth of religious experiences that are part of our lives—experiences that, when shared, become a powerful religious education tool. All of us love stories, and the greatest story that we have to tell is the story of our relationship with God.

Another way of using the person as a medium is through the use of skits or dramatization. Skits based upon scripture or simple themes such as courage, hope or faith could well be employed by religious educators. Involving the teenagers in participatory education gives them the chance to use their own creativity and their own religious experiences as a medium.

Summary

The goal of our effort with our young people is to lead them to adult faith. When people speak of the crisis of faith among teens, I often find myself thinking of the more serious crisis of faith among adults. It is questionable whether teens can come to and survive in faith without the aid of adult communities of living faith. This fact is being highlighted again and again in very recent publications, such as the *National Catechetical Directory* and John Westerhoff's little book, *Will Our Children Have Faith?* More and more it is becoming clear that we need adults who will share the secret of their faith with young people. Programs that avoid that aspect of youth ministry, in my opinion, are doomed to failure. Young people are hungry to experience the holy. Experience of the holy seems to be something that is handed on by people who themselves have experienced it. That's our challenge as adults excited about our treasure called Good News.

The ACEC Experiment: A Multiple-Parish Approach to High School Religious Education

Thomas Zanzig

The following report by Thomas Zanzig of the ACEC Experiment is especially valuable as a detailed description of a specific attempt to develop a catechetical ministry to youth in a particular area. Among many noteworthy aspects of Zanzig's efforts are the careful efforts at laying a groundwork for a program, the successful attempt to involve a variety of adult leaders in planning the overall program, the painstaking attention to detail that went into the preparation of the program, and a recognition that such a program must evolve by allowing for many adaptations and developments over a period of time.

Zanzig has clearly engaged in the experiment called ministry, something much more exciting than merely running a youth program. His vision, found in the following words, challenges all of us who wish to develop improved ministries to young people: "The joy of living, the real challenge of being Christian, is to seek new answers, to discover alternatives, to play with possibilities."
Michael Warren

──────────────── ▲ ────────────────

The problems associated with religious education for public high school students have been so widely discussed and, unfortunately, experienced that it would seem superfluous to review them here in any great detail. Poor attendance, parent apathy, unimaginative programming, difficulties in teacher recruitment, discipline problems, tight money—you name the excuse and just about anyone who has worked on the high school level has used it at one time or another. The real problem is that all the excuses in the world won't relieve us of the responsibility to do something for our adolescents—namely, the responsibility to present Christ and his message to them in a way which maintains the fullness of that message and transmits it in a manner suitable to their needs and abilities. Defining our responsibility is easy, thanks to *The General Catechetical Directory, To Teach As Jesus Did*, the documents of Vatican II, *et al*. Responding to the challenges we confront in trying to live up to that responsibility is another matter.

This article is simply an attempt to share a possible solution, albeit a partial one, for this major catechetical problem we call high school CCD. The solution involves both an organizational structure and a catechetical approach. The concept is proposed not simply as another good idea that someone should try out but rather as a concrete approach which has been tried and tested for five years and, in my opinion, has succeeded remarkably well.

By way of introduction, Appleton, Wisconsin, is a Midwestern city of some sixty thousand people. Economically it is a middle- to upper-income community, politically it is moderate. Theologically, its leaders tend toward liberalism, and the people themselves, for the most part, try hard to follow their lead. Appleton has eight Catholic parishes, seven of which have parochial schools, one Catholic high school, some ten professional religious education coordinators (as of yesterday!) working on the CCD level, only one of whom (me) works on the high school CCD level.

Eight years ago there was no one specifically designated to handle the religious formation of the high school students in Appleton. Each parish "did their own thing," usually unsuccessfully. For the most part associate pastors were responsible for the CCD programs, and though they might be commended for their effort, they generally had little training and even less time to deal effectively with such programs. As a result, volunteer cat-echists did their best with what was available. Those who achieved some measure of success (particularly gifted people) were usually exhausted after a couple of years and went on to choose more "rational" apostolates. Gradually the new phenom-enon of religious education coordinators began to catch on, particularly on the grade school level. But high school CCD pro-grams continued to suffer, until the associate pastors and a number of interested adults decided to do something about the situation.

These concerned leaders got together and analyzed the problem. After long discussions, research and brainstorming of possibilities, the Appleton Catholic Education Council (ACEC) was born in September 1968. Very basically, ACEC is a unified parish effort to provide effective religious formation programs for public high school students. Participating parishes share the financial burden of hiring an executive director for the Council whose responsibility it is to design a program, recruit and train catechists, and attract students. The Council itself, a board of representatives elected and/or appointed by each parish, oversees the operations and programs proposed by the director, promotes the programs on the local parish level, creates and maintains a reasonable budget, and so forth.

Initially ACEC was intended to provide both high school and adult religious education programs. In its first year the bud-get for ACEC was rather arbitrarily set at some $16,800. Five of the eight parishes opted to support the Council and participate in its programs with an individual parish expense based on the size of the parish, number of potential participating students, and so on. After securing corporation status and finalizing a constitu-tion and by-laws, the Council hired its first executive director, an extremely capable and talented man who had the knowledge, vision, and persuasive ability to lay the foundation for ACEC's success.

In 1971 I was hired as the second executive director of ACEC. The first director had moved strongly toward adult edu-cation as the focal point of ACEC's efforts, certainly a valid di-rection considering all the recent rhetoric about the primacy of adult education as the focal point of catechesis. I emphasize the word "rhetoric" simply because it must be admitted that all our talk has not been backed up with a great deal of action in regard to adult catechesis. I agreed to accept the position of director if I would be responsible only for the high school students, a position I took not in disregard of adult education but rather with the conviction that we must begin to hire full-time directors for adult programs if we hope to achieve even moderate success on this level. It is foolhardy to think we can serve our adults effectively when we continue to offer them minimal programs developed by over-worked coordinators with small or non-existent budgets. Incidentally, I am convinced that the multiple-parish approach could well be the key to adult programming for our parishes. My decision to work strictly with high school students was a personal rather than pedagogical one. In any case, the Council accepted my offer and we were on our way.

I came to ACEC with a number of beliefs and convictions about high school catechesis which dictate to a great degree both the organizational structure and the catechetical approach I employ in my programming:

1. *I am firmly convinced that a professional religious educator, meaning one well-grounded in theology and methodology, must be in the room with the students as often as possible if effective religious education is to take place among high school students.* This for two chief reasons. We have a notorious lack of adult volunteers working on the high school level, and those we do have are often (by their own admission) not qualified to deal with high school religious education. Secondly, and relative to the first contention, we need people who can deal with the very difficult questions and attitudes of high school students—questions which include the God question, moral problems, the relevance of religion, and attitudes which can range from that of convinced believers to doubters and professed agnostics and atheists.

2. In order to reach high school students *we must provide programs which are significantly different than any program they've experienced to that point. By that I obviously mean dif-*

ferent content but also different methods, different scheduling, different environments—everything. If, as we profess today, adolescents go through a "negative discovery of self" and, if that development often involves a rejection of attitudes, values, and concepts which are deemed by them to be childish, then it stands to reason that catechetical programs similar to those offered in grade school and even junior high will nearly always be rejected by senior high students.

3. *In religious education we must strive for quality, not quantity.* This assumption is often used to salve the psychological wounds incurred when attendance drops to a new low. But I believe it is equally valid when applied to time—number of classes, length of sessions, etc. I feel that the "one-hour class, once a week" program is doomed before it begins. High school students will take half that hour getting their jackets off. Any real depth of learning is impossible. And volunteer catechists are climbing the walls by Christmas, which of course gives the coordinator *two* major problems—students who are getting nothing out of the program (and telling you so) and volunteers who start getting sick every Wednesday night. We *have* to learn that one well-planned and successful class is far superior to ten lousy ones.

4. *High school students must be approached as young adults seeking real faith, not as turned-off agnostics (or worse) who only want to discuss pre-marital sex, parent-teen relationships, and social problems.* In the last decade I feel many religious educators have totally underestimated our young people, not to mention underestimating the appeal Christ and his message can have for them. When I entered this work some seven years ago, a "successful" coordinator I knew held firmly that we could not mention the word "God" in front of high school students—"you'd lose them all in a week" she told me. I doubted her then; today I'd tell her to get out of the work! I am not denying the value and importance of dealing with so-called "relevant" topics—dating, communication, or identity. In fact these topics form a vital dimension of the program I offer. But we are called to Christianize these dimensions of our lives, and

the only way to do that is to deal with God, Christ, the Church, Christian morality—in other words, with the real guts of our faith.

This contention, if accepted, reinforces my first assumption regarding the need for professional religious educators to teach our high school students. As critical as it may seem, few of our adults are capable of witnessing their faith convictions clearly and forcefully, particularly with teenagers. And yet if God is everything we claim him to be (or, better, if he is everything he tells us he is), then he is precisely what teenagers, like all people, need, want, and are searching for. If we don't respond to *that* need as well as to the social needs of our students, we might not lose them in a week, but we'll have them bored to death after one year. (Have you ever heard this one: "What happened to all those good freshmen we had coming *last* year?" Probable answer —many of them are joining bible study and prayer groups, arguing the God question at parties or discussing the morality of abortion and euthanasia in school.)

On the basis of these assumptions (and others too complex to deal with in this space), I devised the following program. Remember, this is a program offered to *five* parishes and is directed by *one* professional religious educator. Obviously the approach can be adapted readily to varying situations.

For freshmen and sophomores the program consists of the following:

1. Five 2½-hour "Core Sessions" which include the major theological themes we wish to cover. These sessions involve numerous talks, dynamics, discussions, films, etc. which all deal with a given topic approached from a number of different perspectives. All these sessions, in all five parishes, are directed by me with volunteers taking the role of discussion leaders.

2. Five 1½-hour "Follow-Up Sessions" which are conducted by the volunteer catechists following each of the Core Sessions. These sessions are intended either to reinforce material presented in a preceding Core Session or to introduce an upcoming theme. They are far less theological in content than the Core Sessions. The Follow-Ups usually involve a number of simple discussion-starter exercises which can be easily handled by the

volunteers. Because little "heavy" theology is required for these classes, and because the methods used do not involve direct input on the part of the volunteers, the catechists do not experience nearly the apprehension normally associated with high school catechetics.

3. An overnight "Faith Experience Program" is offered to both freshmen and sophomores during the course of the year. Most religious educators are probably familiar with the approach used in such programs, and I'm assuming little explanation is required here. These programs are also directed by myself and priests from our area. They have been remarkably effective in creating a sense of community among the students, reinforcing the major themes covered during the year and, most importantly, solidifying my own relationship with the students.

Therefore any student participating in all that is available to him/her will receive some 33 hours of formal religious education during the year, 26 hours of which will be directly guided by a professional religious educator. I would gladly compare these figures with any other CCD program offered on the high school level.

In order to handle these classes, I teach every Tuesday and Thursday evening of the week, rotating from parish to parish. I therefore get to each parish personally about every six weeks for a Core Session. In the time in between these sessions the volunteers run the Follow-Ups. In this way the students meet about once every three weeks. The program is always new and different, the students are not bored by the normal weekly routine of classes and, as a result, attendance is not only relatively high but remains so—we tend, in fact, to attract *more* students to each successive session during the year.

In our diocese students cannot be confirmed until they have reached their junior year in high school (a point I'd love to spend a great deal more time on here!). As a result the junior program I offer *is* a Confirmation preparation program, consisting of a full weekend faith experience program, four, 2½-hour follow-up sessions, practices, parent meetings, and so forth. I handle this entire program myself with the priests from the parishes participating also. Assuming this situation exists in few dioceses, an approach similar to that used with the freshmen and sophomores could be easily developed for juniors, with the director teaching Core Sessions on Wednesday evenings, which again could be supplemented by Follow-Up Session, faith experiences, etc.

The greatest weakness in our program at present is the senior program. A city-wide approach to these students has been used in the past with little real success. Our Confirmation students are asking for (would you believe *demanding*?) more programs, but I have simply run out of free nights on which to offer such programs. What it amounts to is that we have come to the point of outgrowing ourselves; we have grown to the point now where we have too many students (over 600 last year) needing more than we can offer. As a result I am thinking now of cutting back to three parishes in a year or so in order to have the time necessary to offer an effective senior program on the local parish level.

This growth factor indicates a significant attribute of the multiple parish approach. I view multiple-parish programming as an interim approach to high school catechesis. Initially parishes have (supposedly) too little money to hire individual parish coordinators for the high school level. There is also an attitude in many areas of pessimism regarding the possible success of high school catechesis. The ACEC approach responds to both these factors. With parishes sharing in the expense of the program, arguments about the lack of financial resources are diminished. And if the approach I have outlined here is in fact successful, parishes eventually become more open to expending more money on programs which have proved successful, thus allowing for either an expansion of the city-wide staff or a reduction in the number of parishes for which any one person would be responsible.

I do not, of course, want to give the impression that multiple-parish programming for high school CCD is a cure-all for the myriad problems involved in catechesis at this level. There are still frustrations, there remain problems to be worked out, and the demands placed upon the director by such an approach can be difficult to say the least. However I do feel that this approach offers many pluses, and it would be well for other areas confronting problems similar to those faced in Appleton to consider this approach as a viable alternative.

My final task here is to answer questions which were either raised directly or implied in the preceding overview: How do we form a Council and what is its role? What do we look for in a director for such a program? What can we anticipate in terms of cost? What do the volunteer catechists do—how are they recruited and trained? In addition to answering these basic questions I will also indicate how this approach might be adapted to a wide variety of circumstances and situations.

How Do We Form a Council?

The formation of a properly defined and effective Council is basic to this approach; if it fails to perform properly the entire effort is almost certainly doomed to failure. Any effort that is as broad and far-reaching as the multiple-parish approach to religious education needs a governing body which gives it solidarity, direction, guidance and support. That is the role of the Council. Those who initiate the formation of the Council should do so with the utmost care and thought. I would advise the following:

1. *The Council should consist of at least one key lay member from the local board of education of each participating parish, and a representative number of pastors, associate pastors and/or religious from the parishes involved.* The Council should be large enough to encourage a broad base of input and ideas, but small enough to insure that decision-making is not encumbered by endless debate, argument and discussion. I would recommend nine or eleven members as an ideal, the odd number assuring the avoidance of tie votes during deliberations.

This recommendation is based on the assumption that the participating parishes do in fact have a *total* board of education as opposed to the more restrictive "school board." (If the parish does have only a school board, meaning one totally or for the most part concerned primarily with the parochial school in the parish, it might well be more beneficial to work on alleviating that inadequacy before tackling this endeavor.)

2. It is critical that the members of the Council be drawn from the parish boards of education themselves, rather than from the parish population at large. One of the chief functions of the Council members will be to act as liaisons between the Council and the decision-making bodies in the parish, i.e. pastors, boards of education, parish councils, etc. If they are to fulfill that function, it is essential that the Council members are not only involved and respected members of the parish but also that they have some direct line of communication with its leaders. An almost disastrous mistake, made in the initial years of our Council, was that the members were simply interested adults appointed by the pastors. There were fine people, hard workers, committed Christians. But they had little formal contact with the decision-making bodies in the parish, and communication was extremely weak. As a result ACEC was almost dissolved in its third year simply because the parish councils and boards of education were either unaware of what was being done or were given false information about programs, student response, etc. If the Council members had been representatives from the parish boards of education, they would have been relaying information on a monthly basis directly to the board, the pastor, etc. This line of communication could have avoided or resolved many small problems which reached monumental proportions before our Council even became aware of the fact that a problem existed.

3. The majority of the Council members should be lay representatives; clergy and religious members should constitute the minority. This is not intended in any way to appear anti-clerical. It is simply a matter of practicality. First, if the programs offered by the Council are to be successful they must be supported strongly by the lay people of the parish. A majority of lay members on the Council will help eliminate the attitude of "let Father do it." Secondly, clergy and religious today are for the most part already over-extended and would not be likely to have the time or the energy required adequately to handle an undertaking of this magnitude. And, finally, many dimensions involved in the formation of the Council will require a wide variety

of talents—business and financial acumen, legal counsel, etc.

On a Council of eleven, for example, I would recommend that seven or eight be lay members and three or four be clergy or religious elected by all clergy and religious from participating parishes.

What Does a Council Do?

The Council will first have to clearly define what it hopes to achieve in terms of high school religious education, stating its hopes in clearly defined goals and objectives which will give it direction and purpose. These goals and objectives should be reasonably specific—which parishes are going to participate, which grades are going to be included in the program, how long will it (should it) take to get a program off the ground, etc.? Based on these specifics, a time-line should be constructed to focus the efforts of the Council. On what date should by-laws be ready, articles of incorporation filed, a director hired, etc.?

By-laws governing the powers of the Council, the number, tenure, and qualifications of Council members, terms of office, committees, meeting dates, fiscal calendar—all the affairs of the Council—should be proposed, discussed and finally ratified in order to insure a Council which will not only have direction, purpose and control but, hopefully, longevity. Following the ratification of by-laws the Council should file for legal incorporation with the state government. This is not only helpful but necessary, particularly in the hiring of a director, the paying of salaries and taxes, etc. The Council should also seek tax exempt status from the federal government. All these matters will probably require legal counsel; but they are not very time-consuming and it is quite possible that a lawyer from one of the participating parishes might be enlisted to do this at little or no charge. While all this groundwork is often tedious business, the sharing, joint effort and camaraderie which it requires will in themselves give the Council the initial solidarity it requires for success.

Hiring the Director

The most critical decision the Council will have to make is the selection of its Executive Director, the person responsible for the actual creation of programs, recruitment of teachers, promotion, etc. The type of individual required will obviously be dictated by the goals which the Council has set for itself. What I recommend is based on the assumption (a debatable one at that!) that the Council will have in mind the kind of program I offer for ACEC.

The critical factor, it seems to me, is whether the Council wishes a person who is primarily an administrator and teacher-trainer or one who will be working directly with the students a great deal as I do. To some degree the talents and characteristics are the same regardless of the role the executive director will play, but there are subtle differences:

1. In either case the executive director must have a solid background in theology and education. Specific training in religious education as a particular field of study is preferred, but a theology background with some practical teaching experience would be acceptable.

2. The individual must obviously be committed to the faith and able to share it with others.

3. He or she must exhibit administrative talents. Though the Council members may well be able to handle the financial affairs, for example, the director must be able to devise adequate budgets, keep records, develop a library of resources, etc.

4. The director must be capable of relating to all age groups effectively. Here is where we see one of the subtle factors which become important in selecting a director. If the Council desires someone who can design a program and train catechists to teach it, it will be looking primarily for an *adult* educator who knows how to work with students. The director would spend the greater part of the time with the catechists; it is essential that the rapport between the two be considered of paramount importance. If, however, the Council desires one who will be in the room with the students as often as possible, it will be looking primarily for a *high school teacher* who knows how to work with adults. It

remains questionable what constitutes a good high school teacher, but deciding this basic question will give the Council some indications as to the age, appearance, personality, practical experience, etc., which it would desire in its executive director.

5. The director should be hired initially with a one-year contract in order to give both parties a chance to work with and evaluate each other. If an extension of the contract is desired after the first year, I strongly recommend a *minimum* contract of three years. It will take at least that long to develop an effective program. The director must be assured of the continued support of the parishes, and the parishes in turn must know that they can rely on the on-going commitment of the director.

6. *Note well:* If the Council begins by hiring a director, as I recommend, it should *not* dictate directly the content nor the kind of program to be offered. This is the role of the director, and it is vital that he or she be free to utilize his or her own talents in developing a program. On the other hand, the Council should feel free to define the kind of program it desires and then seek a director who would accept and support such an approach. But it should not first hire a director and then tell him or her what to provide.

What Can We Anticipate In Terms of Cost?

The greatest expense involved in any program of this kind is, of course, the salary of the director. In terms of the demands of the job and the qualifications which are required in a director for such a program, I would suggest considering a minimum salary of $12,000, varying to some degree according to local cost of living, relative salaries given other teachers in the area, etc. To some this may seem high, to others low. The point is that the salary offered must seem not only just but appealing if the Council hopes to hire a properly qualified individual.

Most of the other factors involved in setting a budget are relative to the program the director will offer, the number of students who will participate, available resources, etc. Will secretarial help be required and how much will it cost? Will an office have to be provided or is one available and furnished? What fringe benefits will the director receive—car allowance, medical insurance, retirement benefits? All of these are questions which must be answered. Remember also that many of these items will not vary significantly regardless of the number of parishes involved. A salary in this range will be required whether three or five parishes participate. Fringe benefits will remain the same. The only significant fluctuating figure involved is the cost of the actual program materials which, compared to such large items as salary and fringe benefits, is relatively small. Film rentals, for example, will not affect the budget a great deal regardless of the number of parishes involved.

From my own experience I would suggest an initial budget proposal of $20,000. This would likely be more than adequate and it might well be reduced after one year's experience. But it is most helpful to allot too much the first year rather than too little.

What about the Volunteer Catechists?

The approach I have outlined does not eliminate nor reduce the need for volunteer catechists; it does, however, redefine their role. Assuming again that we are talking about a program similar to mine, there are a number of points to be made:

1. Regarding the recruitment of catechists, the executive director of a multiple-parish program will not be in a position to do this effectively, at least not initially. Not only is it likely that the director will be new to the area and unfamiliar with the people in the parishes, but he or she will also not be directly linked to any one parish though responsible for many. As a result, the recruitment of teachers initially will have to be the responsibility of pastors, associate pastors or, less likely, the board of education. The pastors and associates are theoretically the most qualified for this task in that they know the people and the students and can best determine who would be appropriate.

2. The qualifications required in a catechist have been well documented elsewhere and I hesitate to review them here. It is

important to mention, however, that in a program similar to mine, in which the director plays such a vital teaching role, the chief characteristics needed by a volunteer catechist would be: (a) A commitment to the faith and the ability to witness Christian convictions, and (b) a love for this age group and the ability to relate well with high school students.

The catechist need not, in other words, be skilled in teaching techniques or capable of giving formal talks on theological topics. It is assumed that the director would train interested adults to fit the needs dictated by the program.

3. As an aside, one of the great advantages to the program structure I propose is the fact that it demands far less of adult volunteers than other high school religion programs. As a result, catechists are not only more easily recruited but there is a far smaller annual turnover of teachers. The vast majority of my volunteers have worked with me for three years or more. To some degree this is a sign, I hope, that they feel a commitment to me personally and that we have formed real friendship over the years. But equally important, I feel, is the fact that they are not threatened by their role and have grown truly to enjoy sharing with the students. Incidentally, the fact that the director leads many of the programs means that fewer catechists would be required than is normally the case.

Adaptability of This Approach

I believe that the two basic elements of this approach are both adaptable to other situations. For example, the pattern of *fewer but longer sessions* for high school students would be valid even in a single parish situation. The director's free time could be used for counselling individual students, running social-service and recreational projects, etc. And might not this same pattern be valid even within Catholic high schools? Should our Catholic high schools attempt to have their religion classes scheduled and conducted like other classes, or be significantly different, as I suggested in the first section of this report.

Again, if a parish (or parishes) simply cannot afford to hire a professional religious educator, a parish priest could much more easily lead such a program, because of the greatly reduced number of sessions. Also, volunteer catechists could more easily team-teach such a program because they would have three full weeks between sessions to prepare adequately.

And, with regard to the multiple-parish Council structure, might it not be suitable for grade school, family-centered, and adult programs? Could there be an answer here for smaller rural communities which cannot afford their individual parish coordinators?

The questions and possibilities seem endless as always. The joy of living, the real challenge of being Christian is to seek new answers, to discover alternative, to play with possibilities. That's what I've done, and I hope my experience may prove beneficial for others.

Understanding the
Weekend Format

Michael Warren

The article that follows is an attempt to understand and appreci-
ate the rapid development of youth retreats in the United States,
by situating this weekend approach with the context of recent
trends in the catechetical ministry to young people in the United
States. The writer wishes to encourage those who have been running these Weekends of Christian Living to trust their own experience and recognize that they are not engaged in a fad but
rather in a significant development in the Church's ministry to
youth.

▲

Chroniclers of the American catechetical scene in the 1960's
and 1970's will have to note the dramatic growth of the weekend
retreat as a specially useful format for the development of faith.
My own relationship with these team-centered weekends has
been a happy one, in spite of difficulties at the beginning. In
1964, when Fathers Douglas Brown and James Tugwood of
Brooklyn began the Christian Awakening program for teens,
their radical move away from the silent monastic-type retreats so
common in Catholic high schools caused some consternation.
Skeptics told them they were engaging in faddism and were developing a program certain to fizzle fast. However, just the opposite has happened. That program and others like it have been
growing steadily ever since. Moreover, in my own development,
I now see that working on these weekends has, more than any

other single factor, shaped my own understanding of the tasks of
adolescent catechesis.

My purpose here is threefold: to put these youth retreats,
which I prefer to call "Christian Experience Programs," into the
context of the current situation of adolescent catechesis in the
United States; to give some reasons for the popularity and success of these programs at the present time; and to reflect on
some of the problem areas that have surfaced in this important
aspect of youth ministry.

The Situation of Adolescent Catechesis

In the recent past, adolescent catechesis has fallen on hard
times. A few years ago the Diocese of Cleveland published ten-
year statistics on CCD attendance by teens, which many found
to be representative of what was happening in dioceses far from
Ohio. In 1964, 31% of Cleveland adolescents, grades 9-12, were
in CCD programs; 33% were in Catholic high schools, and 36%
were involved in no catechetical programs at all. In 1973, those
in Catholic high schools had fallen from 33% to 21%; those in
CCD programs had fallen from 31% to 16%; and those in no catechetical programs of any kind had jumped from 36% to a whop-
ping 63%.

A survey conducted by the Department of Education at the
United States Catholic Conference in 1974 showed the Cleveland
statistics were generally valid for the entire country. Almost all
respondents to the survey questionnaire noted that attendance at
catechetical programs for teens was down. However, while acknowledging serious problems and even widespread discouragement in their dioceses, more than half the respondents saw
signs of hope in two developments. One of these was the gradual
emergence of a comprehensive ministry to youth. The other was
the growth of the youth retreat movement.

Retreat/Christian Experience Weekends

Without exception, where retreat-type programs were mentioned, they were given as examples of successful programs.

These programs have a variety of names and formats. The most common ones mentioned were Search and Teens Encounter Christ. Since young people themselves are members of retreat teams in many dioceses, several respondents saw the retreat movement at least in part as a ministry of youth to youth. One might conclude that in some areas retreats are no longer looked on as adjunct elements in catechetical work but as a core element in youth catechesis.

What this U.S.C.C. questionnaire tells me is that, far from being a fad for 1964, retreat-type programs for youth are more and more answering a need expressed by young people. These programs are growing all over the country. More and more dioceses are getting involved in one or another type of Christian Experience Weekend program.

Information from the written questionnaire was backed up in regional meetings held in 1975 with representatives from over a hundred and fifty dioceses. One of the items of agenda for those meetings was the following question: "What kinds of catechetical programs for adolescents have been most successful in your diocese?" Overwhelmingly, the programs currently offering the greatest satisfaction and success in dioceses represented at the meetings were those that have evolved out of a retreat model. These programs have a variety of formats, especially of weekend formats. In many cases the basic weekend program has been adapted to two-day, one-day, or shorter time segments more suitable for young teens.

That, then, in brief is the current situation of adolescent catechesis as I've been able to determine it. It underlines the important place of Christian Experience Programs in current work with teens. But why are these weekend programs so successful? Is it possible to account for the growing success of these programs at the very time when other attempts to work with youth are experiencing growing failure? I believe it is possible. As I see it, the success of these programs stems from the solid theological and cultural presuppositions on which they are based. Let us examine these somewhat briefly.

Search, Teens Encounter Christ, The Christian Awakening, COR weekends—all these programs and those similar to them rest on a theological presupposition that Jesus is present in the life of each person. What happens in the process of conversion is that a person recognizes that the Christian message is the answer to one's own deepest hopes and longings. When one discovers that the Christian mystery makes sense of the absurdity of life, then one is ripe either for conversion or for another step in one's response to that mystery. These programs have great confidence in the power of the gospel to speak even to those who profess to be non-believers.

Actually these Christian Experience Programs are affirming something Karl Rahner said several years ago ("The Significance of the Individual Member," *Christian Commitment*, pp. 102-103):

Christianity has to grow from its own principle of life. Of course, it also has to be transmitted to men from outside. But it would be a false understanding of what preaching is, whether by the authoritative *magisterium* or the pastor in his official work, to suppose that it can or should transmit Christianity to a man as though he were, at best, an empty hollow space ready and waiting for it, or a schoolboy learning of Australia for the first time in a geography lesson. The grace of God has always been there ahead of our preaching; a man is always in a true sense a Christian already when we begin to commend Christianity to him. For he is a man, already included in God's general will for salvation, redeemed by Christ, with grace already living and working in his innermost heart at least as the proffered possibility of supernatural action. Hence, our preaching is not really an indoctrination with something alien from outside but the awakening of something within, as yet not understood but nevertheless really present; something that is not, of course, to be misunderstood in the modernist sense as a natural religious need in the human subconscious, but which is a grace of God.

Any approach to a man in words from outside, if it is Christian, is always an appeal to God who is already speaking by grace within him and being in some sense heard; any communication of Christianity is always a communication of what is already there, alive, within a man. And if it often seems to be otherwise, if people get the impression that we are preaching a very extraordinary, remote doctrine, intelligible only to experts, which no normal man could find interesting unless he stopped being an ordinary man, it is not because Christianity is really like this but because we have not rightly understood it.

What Rahner describes as the process of leading the individual to faith could easily be applied to the group process on our weekends. What happens so often is that the group that begins as a more or less loose gathering grows to become a dynamic community of faith. The Gospel ceases to be a word from outside the group's life and becomes rather a word reflecting the inner life of the group itself. I myself have seen intense excitement generated by the scripture readings at Mass, when those present recognized that their own group experience authenticated the truth of the gospel. I like to call communal experiences like these "Emmaus experiences," because like the disciples in Luke's account, group members recognize that Jesus has been present in their midst, even though they vaguely realized it at the time.

As almost a digression, I would like to point out that the kind of doctrinal understandings attained through such experiences of a community of faith tend to be well-integrated and profound, and we should not apologize for them. What we are doing is getting back to the practice of the early Church, where it was presumed that the most effective grasp of the Christian message could be gotten from the actual life of the community of believers. We must avoid the mistake of categorizing these weekends as experiences of community, as if they were not at the same time experiences of doctrinal realities of our faith. One diocese I know of has a policy of making Search available to all its teens as an experience of community. In addition, each young person must attend twenty-five hours of doctrinal instruction. What bothers me about such a policy is that it over-compartmentalizes Search as an experience of community. Community and doctrine are not so neatly separate, especially in a well-run weekend of Christian living. That policy would be fine so long as we recognize that the weekend experience itself is an experience of doctrinal realities, but as a much more direct and possibly vital way than by merely abstracting from them. As I see it, these weekends provide the best contexts for sound doctrinal instruction. But more about this aspect later.

There are cultural reasons why these programs are succeeding at a time of catechetical malaise. First, these programs deal with the problem of the statuslessness of the young. Teenagers are at a point in life where they feel capable of shouldering responsibilities but at the same time find themselves excluded from having any real say in the life of their churches. As a result they drop out. At least such is one of the conclusions reached by Merton Strommen in *A Study of Generations*, his recent study of Lutheran church members.

Strommen found that for most youth there is a sense of being on the outside of their congregation's interests and life. Over half the youth he surveyed (aged 15-23) felt that older people in the congregation were suspicious of them. They also felt that they had no influence on the decisions being made by the congregation. In other words, the institutional life of the congregation has evolved in such a way that leadership and influence are in the hands of people over thirty. Up to one-half of the youth agree that "hardly anyone in the congregation would miss me if I stopped going." Strommen says, "We found that the strongest predictor of youth's attitude toward his church is how well he fits in with groups in his congregation. The acceptance that he feels is the best indication of how he will evaluate his congregation."

Programs like Search are dealing directly with this problem of the statuslessness of young people. They provide adolescents with a communal life within which they have an indispensable role. These programs offer the young an opportunity to develop their own ministry to their peers and beyond their peers. It is no wonder young people who are looking to be taken seriously are solidly committed to these programs that put them into a central role. I suspect that in some parts of the country, Christian Experience Programs are forcing parish CCD programs to make much greater use of the young people themselves in planning and running weekly CCD session. As far as I can determine, where such participation is encouraged, CCD is in pretty good shape.

A second cultural reason why Christian Experience Programs are succeeding is that they provide the kind of on-going dialogue needed for the maintenance of the process of conversion. In their book *The Social Construction of Reality*, sociologists Peter Burger and Thomas Luckmann point out that the crucial part of the conversion process is not the actual moment of conversion, but the on-going process of maintaining the new (or renewed) world-view of the person converted. They hold that conversion involves a new way of approaching reality and the acceptance of new values. The convert begins to inhabit a different universe of meaning. The maintenance of this new world is achieved through on-going conversation and dialogue.

Most of the Christian Experience Programs I know about encourage those who have been on one weekend to come back to others in one or another capacity. There is a whole system of renewal that many of us refer to as follow-up. Reunions, second-level weekends, and training programs are all means by which to assist the young in maintaining and even growing beyond their original Christian Experience Weekend. Further, these programs foster a network of relationships within which conversation about faith can be maintained. All of us have to shoulder the burden of what can happen if we fail to make provision for these follow-up programs: the final state may be worse and more disillusioned than their original state.

Obviously I feel very strongly about the value of these programs, a value that is becoming obvious to more and more people each year. As I see things developing, these programs are going to become even more important in the future than they are today. As a way of helping us face the future and begin to improve our programs, I'd like to suggest the following six aspects of the programs for greater attention and for some improvement.

1. The first aspect needing continued attention is the Christ-centeredness of our programs. Being together for a weekend in an atmosphere of love and caring would most probably produce

a keen sense of community among the participants. Such a community would probably also be a community of faith, that is, of faith in oneself, and in one another. As leaders of our programs, we want, must have, that kind of root human faith, but I think we must actively pursue a further goal of becoming a community of faith in Christ. To pursue such a goal means that the directors and team-members must have a keen sense of the power and presence of the Lord in their own lives and in their work with youth. To do less is to be inauthentic. It is to mask the Christ-centeredness of our motivation and to settle for a weekend of communication skills and/or group therapy. My point is that we know there is more. Here I go along with Rahner that the greatest of gifts to man is that of being consciously Christian.

I realize that to keep our program Christ-centered demands that in fact our motivation and lives be actually centered on Jesus. Yes, that is the hard part about catechesis. There is no way to pass the gospel on credibly to others—to pass it on as good news—except as it has meant something in our own personal lives. Nobody wants a disembodied gospel; it is ridiculous, unbelievable, incredible, uncredible. The hard part of catechesis for all of us is that whether we like it or not, we ourselves must somehow embody deep faith in Christ. The gospel becomes most real when it is inscribed in a life and not just in a book. Especially with our teenage team members we must make our faith in Christ very explicit so they will be encouraged to make their own faith explicit.

2. Second, we have to pay special attention to the freedom-centeredness of our programs. If we are not careful, they can easily become manipulative. I think adult leaders in these programs should be preoccupied with freedom. Some weekends can be so high-powered, especially when the group or communal process gets rolling, that some individuals can be effectively denied a chance to disagree or perceive differently. Not all the kids are at the same place when they come; why should we expect them all to be at the same place when they leave. Not even all the team members can be expected to be at the same place.

In my experience, it is the teenager team members who

must be reminded again and again about the issue of freedom. They have to be taught to reverence the rhythm of growth in individual lives. Older, more experienced team members probably have less trouble with this matter. However, I have met many teenage team members who are so concerned about the success of the weekend that they find it difficult to tolerate differences or the person who won't go along. The whole area of freedom is a matter we adults must be right on top of during our weekends. If at the start we have in our minds some sort of pre-set response we expect from each youngster, then we are already off on the wrong footing.

3. Third, I'd like to call attention to the need for good adult input on our weekends. Some may disagree with this idea, especially since some Search programs are exclusively peer-to-peer. However, I myself believe that such weekends are excellent opportunities to make simple and clear presentations of core aspects of the Christian mystery. And I believe that these matters should be presented by well-qualified and well-prepared adults. I am not speaking here of abstracted truths. I'm speaking of presentations dominated by witness and filled with the kind of personal examples we have all found so effective in these programs.

Let me restate this point. I do not believe that all the presentations on a Christian Experience Weekend should be given by teen team members. Possibly two-thirds of the formal presentations should be given by teens, while the remaining third should be given by adults who have worked out, with help from appropriate consultants, clear and personal explanations of central aspects of the Christian message. Our weekends are the right time to give such input, when it can be discussed and then later integrated into worship and other activities. Nor are such presentations merely pasted onto a weekend experience. They must be integral, pointing to the significance of what all are experiencing on the weekend.

In this connection, it seems crucial that all presentations given by teen team members should be reviewed beforehand by members of the team, especially by the adult members. Otherwise we run the danger of having glib, carelessly prepared team members. I know this matter requires time. However, the alternative is a poorly run program.

4. A fourth area for consideration is that of evaluation. Evaluation is becoming more and more an accepted part of modern life. Evaluation, long an accepted practice in industry and education, is becoming more important in the other professions. It is possible that many of us have had first-hand experience of the usefulness of the regional educational association's evaluation of a school. Such an evaluation forces all in the school to sharpen up their performance and face up to hidden weaknesses. It might be helpful if we made it our business to have outsiders come in once a year to one of our programs and evaluate it according to criteria agreed upon beforehand. It might be ideal if the evaluators were connected with an entirely different-type program, say, having someone from a Teens Encounter Christ (TEC) program evaluate Search in your diocese. At any rate, we can find Search evaluators from the Search program in a neighboring diocese. In my experience, these programs can be so satisfying or even exhilarating to the adult leaders that we can easily grow complacent and blind to the need for our programs to grow and improve.

5. Fifth, I see a need for some kind of sharing among leaders of the different Christian Experience models. The whole youth retreat movement appears to me to be growing rapidly. The leaders should be getting together, sharing organizational problems, and swapping ideas for new developments. Exactly how much sharing is to take place, I am not certain. I feel certain that such sharing will never take place without (1) the direction of talented leadership and (2) the careful avoidance of rivalry, jealousy, and suspicions. The healthiest sign of the youth retreat movement in my opinion is exactly the kind of variety that has grown up in these programs throughout this country. Our motto must be: "Encourage all initiatives." There are so many young people needing our services that no one program, be it Search or TEC or COR or Christian Awakening, can take care of them all. Search is not the last word in Christian Experience Programs. There is no last word. All our programs should

be seen as beginnings. In addition, the true sign of the professional is his respect for fellow professionals and his eagerness to learn from them. So, this weekend you might want to discuss a broader kind of sharing.

6. Finally, let us give more attention to the parents of our young people. I think we should be in touch with them and make ourselves available to them. Obviously, we have only limited time and we can't do everything. It is just that this may be the one thing we cannot afford to leave undone. Let the kids themselves plan the program for parents and then run it. We all know stories about what happens when there is a clash in the home over Search. Such clashes are painful for all. I'm not certain they are always necessary. Sometimes the parents need a taste of the very kind of experience the kids had on one of the weekends. Well, we may want to consider how to provide it for them.

In conclusion, all of us in this ministry have much cause for joy. Our work is making a difference in the lives of many young people. And, yes, we ourselves are making a difference in those lives. We can all imagine how much poorer our lives would have been if we never had the chance to do this work. That's what we all have to rejoice over: that we have been called to a privileged ministry.

Part III

Leadership Development

Christian Experience Weekends: Role of the Director

Michael Warren

A large majority of the young adults now seeking full-time ministry in various dioceses of this country have come to ministry, not through the hothouse training programs of seminaries and novitiates but rather through years of in-service apprenticeship on youth retreat teams. Through these teams they grew in their own sense of and developed considerable skills for ministry. Often enough, in the background of this development are those who direct these weekend programs. They are the ones responsible for nurturing the seeds of ministry within so many young people. Theirs has been the specially privileged role of being "ministers to the ministers."

The following article speaks directly to those responsible for the direction of these weekend programs. Even though some of the material in this article overlaps with that in the previous piece on the weekend format, it is included here because it attempts to summarize some of the principles and caveats that have been shared with the writer over a period of years by dozens of directors of such programs. The true value of these weekend programs for any diocese goes far beyond their value for a particular group of young people participating in a weekend program. That value lies rather in the success of such programs in developing the leadership needed for authentic ministry in today's Church.

▲

Christian Experience Programs are continuing to develop in the United States as is evidenced by the two well-designed faith experience weekends in the high school catechetical program of the Green Bay Plan, and by the spread of older programs like the Search Program, Teens Encounter Christ, and the Christian Awakening of the Brooklyn Diocese. As Christian experience programs continue to expand, a key person continues to be the director of these weekends. In the following pages, I want to focus especially on his role while at the same time:

1. outlining the characteristics of these programs, using as one model, the Brooklyn based Christian Awakening Program;

2. showing that these programs are in accord with the thrust of modern catechetical theory;

3. treating five special problems that should concern a youth director in developing new programs.

What is a Christian experience program? Actually "Christian experience program" is an umbrella expression used to cover a wide variety of programs that have sprung up over the past ten years. They follow naturally from developments in personalist psychology, and communications theory, and from pastoral efforts like the Cursillo. Although these programs can be of a single day's or even of only several hours' duration, most of them resemble retreats. They involve a substantial period of time spent in a group considering matters of personal faith development. Unlike retreats of old, the talks are not given by any one person; instead the program is run by a team, often comprised of both adults and teenagers. Even though these programs make use of formal presentations or talks, the emphasis is rather on activity, on discussion and interaction among those making the program. The topics of these presentations and discussions might include: the meaning of our relationship to the Trinity (grace); the role of the sacraments in Christian life; the place of prayer; the functions of Christian leadership; obstacles to God's friendship, and the role of the community in Christian living. Even though all talks tend to be of a high calibre theologically, emphasis is on witness, that is, on the christian mystery as it is revealed in the living document of a person's life. Emphasis is also on the community or group and on concrete learning rather than on some master or teacher and vertically imposed abstractions.

In the Christian education of the young, I believe that these programs are the way of the future. The reasons are numerous.

Young people are painfully conscious of the need for relationship and these programs meet their need.

These programs are well suited to the nature of the christian message. In the early church, groups met to talk over "the events of recent days" and in so doing, came to discover the Risen Lord in their midst.

These programs are successful at a time when other catechetical efforts with the young are falling apart at the seams, both on this continent and in Europe.

The programs fit in with recent catechetical theory, especially as it has been developing since 1960.

Four dominant themes in modern catechetical theory are also reflected in christian experience programs: These are (1) the centrality of the group, (2) the importance of context, (3) the principle of adaptation, and (4) the centrality of Christ.

Centrality of the Group. Paragraphs 76 and 87 of the *General Catechetical Directory* state, "For adolescents and young adults, the group must be considered a vital necessity. In a group, the adolescent or the young adult comes to know himself and finds support and stimulation." (76) The conclusions of the 1971 International Catechetical Congress held in Rome also emphasize the importance of groups. This is a rather new emphasis. All of us can think back to youth retreats which set kids in neat rows of pews for talks, before sending them out alone and in silence to reflect on what they heard. At the same time, meals in silence attempted to keep the group physically together while stifling group interaction. Today, however, stress is placed on tapping the dynamic of the group, encouraging it to function in a healthy and open way. We have finally come to trust groups and the healing and educative value of group learning.

In most programs, the basic principle in operation is this: a group influences a group. Thus the team members themselves come together prior to the weekend for meetings totaling six to eight hours, so that they can form a group or community of prayer, reflection, and work. Together they attempt to come to agreement on their common goals in serving those who will be making the weekend program for the first time.

During the weekend itself the team attempts to be seen as a community of faith, prayer, and service to others. The participants are broken into several stable subgroups, and two team members are assigned to each of these. Since the group itself is central, these team members do not function as discussion leaders but rather strive to function as fully as possible as peer group members.

This process places the youth director in a new role where authority is more horizontal than vertical, for the director is not the only person in the group knowledgeable about matters of faith. The director's is to be more "the leadership of the closed mouth" rather than pronouncements from "on high." Far from being the star of the weekend, he/she must earn the privilege of entering into the total group or any sub-group. Such a role demands particularly good balance and group sense. I presume that not all diocesan youth directors can function in such a role; thus the weekend director may very well be different from the diocesan director. The diocesan director may see his/her job as identifying personnel who can function with this crucial sort of horizontal leadership.

Role of Context. In our past catechetical efforts we have not always recognized the importance of the context in which learning takes place. We have been largely unaware that all learning takes place in situations. All learning is contextual. The *Directory* states, "They (catechists) are responsible for choosing and creating suitable conditions which are necessary for the Christian message to be sought, accepted, and more profoundly investigated." (71)

In a Christian experience program much attention is given to atmosphere and environment. This is because learning does not come from any one person's word but more from the total context of openness, freedom, care and service. The youth director and team foster the climate of openness chiefly by listening and by attuning themselves to the individuals in sub-groups. If freedom is to be another characteristic of these programs the youth director will have to encourage teen team members to resist any tendency to exert pressure on the participants that might impair the freedom needed for real growth. Finally, the team needs to show in subtle and astonishing ways, the same sort of delicate caring and service which mark Christ's washing of his disciples' feet. Eventually, the team creates a climate of openness and receptivity in which participants can relax enough to consider the most important issues of their lives.

Principle of Adaption. Central to current catechetical thought is the principle of adaptation: The Christian mystery is radically a message for man, a source of joy for him, if only it be communicated so as to shed light on his experience. The possible adaptations of the message are as numerous as are the varied situations and experiences of persons. Among the most effective catechesis I have seen have been the carefully worked out presentations made to young people on these weekends—at times by young persons close to their own age.

This principle of adaptation is especially seen in the use of language. The message is given in language that young people can understand. But there is another angle to the question of language, and here the director's role is a crucial and ticklish one. Because these programs are based on a principle of dialogue, they attempt to allow faith to find its own language. When that happens one can expect to hear young people speak excitedly of the christian mystery in their own words. What I see going on in these situations is something profoundly significant; it is faith seeking a language. I believe that most young people have faith, but they do not possess the words with which to articulate that faith. In these programs young people try to define a new language for faith.

Centrality of Christ. In general, my measure of the worth of a Christian experience program is this: How Christ-centered is it? Catechesis has launched its renewal precisely on the issue of centering the message in the person of Jesus Christ, and not on dissected creed, code or cult. "What we preach is Christ and him crucified." Unfortunately we all have that very human tendency to put first things fifth or ninth or to neglect them altogether. We face this same danger in our catechetical programs. We can get caught up in our group dynamics or with our theology and some-how lose focus on Christ. I believe that conscious allegiance to Jesus Christ is one of the great gifts of human existence, and the youth director must ask himself if he is comfortable and willing to share his own faith openly with others.

In sharing our faith in Christ, it is not a question of giving participants the impression that we have arrived. We can be honest in admitting that we are in process of renewing our faith search again and again. And as happens in so many new tes-tament resurrection accounts, the Lord appears to those who puzzle over him or search for him. Hopefully one of the out-comes of a christian experience program will be a deep under-standing of the presence of the Risen Lord in the midst of a com-munity of faith.

Even though these Christian experience programs are quite in line with current catechetical thinking, they are not without problems and dangers. Let us look at five of these problems. The first is the lack of a critical sense. It is all too easy in such pro-grams to become self-satisfied with our efforts, because they seem to have such an impact on those they serve. Yet, if these programs are to be truly effective they must be continually eval-uated with such questions as: Was the team careful to respect the freedom of those making the retreat program? Were the talks well-prepared? Did the team work well together? Was the week-end Christ-centered? Was the program concerned about the next step for the participants, i.e., carrying over some of what they learned into their everyday lives? Was an opportunity offered for individual counseling with a qualified adult?

A second problem in these programs is the lack of follow-up. Sometimes a weekend experience can help youngsters to become more deeply conscious of their own feelings and thoughts, but they scarcely have time to assimilate all they expe-rience. They will need some kind of support if they are to stave off discouragement when they return home. Or sometimes a young person may have confided for the first time thoughts of suicide or homosexual fears. Such a person may need only a few more sessions of counseling to be set straight or he/she may need referral to a therapist. Follow-up is so important that it makes necessary the following rule of thumb. If there is to be no follow-up, it would be better to have no program.

Tied to follow-up is the problem of preparation and training. As in good baseball, good ballet, good writing, good anything, the secret of success is careful preparation. There is no substitute for it, especially for teenage team members. Any preparation takes time. That is why any director working with these programs must be ready and able to give the kind of time it demands.

A fourth problem is that of unrealistic expectations. The secret to achieving goals is to limit them. A weekend program is one experience in the total life of an individual. It does not have to accomplish everything—because it cannot. I do not want to deny that one of these programs can have a very significant influence on a person's life; I do want to deny that it is likely the influence will be total. We will let ourselves in for many unnecessary disappointments as youth directors if we do not understand realistically the limitations of our efforts.

The final problem is the one I am most concerned about. It is that of not being in touch with the parents of our young people who make these programs. I am not saying that in order to run experience centered programs you have to take on the entire pastoral ministry of the Church. It is just that today more than ever before, we owe it to parents to keep them informed about what we are doing. For example, I should think that sometimes after a weekend experience, the young people should be invited to come with their parents to meet the directors of the program and hear from them a description of what the program was like. It might be that the parents could be encouraged to participate in experience-centered programs for adults, such as the Cursillo or Marriage Encounter. I should think that having some adult lay people, possibly parents, on a youth program would be most desirable. The point is that we are kidding ourselves if we think that the faith crisis today is most acute among the teenage crowd. Crises of adult proportions are to be found among adults.

Whatever the risks and problems of attempting to run experience-centered programs, they are worth the effort, in fact the field is wide open for new imaginative efforts along these lines and at many different levels. Experimental formats should be tried with junior high students, as well as with those of college age and with adults. Follow-up weekends of greater depth for those who have already been through one weekend are also needed. Whatever further developments are to come in this area, we can expect they will come from leaders who possess faith, vision, and a deep sense of care.

Some Information Resources

1. For information on sophomore and senior faith experience weekends:
Green Bay Plan
Diocesan Department of Education
133 South Monroe Avenue, P.O. Box 186
Green Bay, Wis. 54305

2. For information on Search for Christian Maturity Program:
National CYO Federation
1312 Massachusetts Ave., N.W.
Washington, D.C. 20005

3. For information on The Christian Awakening Program (including CBS film on Awakening, *I'm Nobody, Who Are You?*):
St. Paul's Center
484 Humboldt St.
Brooklyn, N.Y. 11211

4. For a variety of weekend formats and models:
Office of Youth Retreats
Diocese of Richmond
813 Cathedral Place
Richmond, Va. 23220

Effective Ministry to Youth

Merton P. Strommen

One of the leading American researchers of youth's attitudes is Lutheran sociologist Merton P. Strommen. The following section is excerpted from Strommen's little book *Five Cries of Youth* (New York: Harper and Row, 1974), a report of research done among more than seven thousand young people, representing a variety of Christian denominations and a sampling of non-churched youth. The "cries of youth" heard by Strommen in his research are: The Cry of Self-Hatred, The Cry of Psychological Orphans, The Cry of Social Protest, The Cry of the Prejudiced, and The Cry of the Joyous. Though highly interpretative, Strommen's book is filled with insights valuable to parents and all others active in ministry to young people.

The section presented here describes the attitudes of effective leaders working with young people and suggests some basic stances local parishes might take toward youth. Strommen's ideas could be the basis of a fruitful discussion among those concerned about youth in any of our Catholic parishes.

Michael Warren

——————————— ▲ ———————————

How Effective Leaders Approach Youth

How does one reach out in a helping relationship to youth?

The persons best qualified to answer this question are youth leaders who themselves excel in reaching out. In order to hear what they say, we first had to locate the cream of the crop.

Through a study conducted in 1970, we developed criteria for effective youth leaders. Once the criteria were ranked, we asked the heads of national youth organizations to nominate leaders of high-school youth who exemplify some of the highest ranked criteria.

Ninety-one youth leaders were named by the following groups: American and Southern Baptist (10); Roman Catholic (6); Christian Church (9); Church of God (9); Evangelical Covenant (7); Episcopal (4); American and Missouri Synod Lutheran (21); United Methodist (6); Greek Orthodox (2); United Presbyterian (1); and Young Life (16). The ninety-one workers then told, through questionnaries, why they intervene in the lives of youth, how they approach them, and what accounts for their effectiveness.

Motives. The first of three questions put to the workers was: Why do you intervene in the lives of young people—that is, what contribution do you feel that you can make to their lives?

As might be expected, over half the respondents cited religious motives: "I want to share my faith," "I can guide them to a full Christian commitment," and the like.

Virtually all, in some part of their free responses, used a desire to influence youth in directions consonant with the Christian way of life as their predominant motive. And this motive clearly arose out of love, concern, and profound respect for youth.

Many responses showed that the leaders were keenly sensitive to the autonomy of youth and committed to techniques which would not violate it. Thus, they did not speak of evangelizing youth, controlling their environment, supervising their behavior, preaching the gospel to them, or other tactics that might be interpreted as applying pressure. Instead they made statements like "I can listen," "I can communicate," "I can be a friend," "I can be a significant adult in their lives," and "I can share my happiness."

A number of insightful youth leaders also recognized that their motivation includes self-realization. "They contribute to my goals." "They keep me young." "I can learn from them." But there was no evidence of self-aggrandizement at the expense of youth, only self-fulfillment as a consequence of helping others develop their potential.

Methods. Three questions were directed to the skills exercised by successful church youth workers. The first question was: What ways of approaching youth have you found helpful? How do you get next to them? Responses revealed six groups of skills:

1. Building Relationships
   Knowing them—home life, school, friends
   Exhibiting deep, sensitive, personal concern for them
   Showing them courtesy
   Participating with them as an equal
   Showing appreciation for a job well done
   Helping them if they ask
   Sharing mutual experiences
   Sharing my own feelings about life
2. Being Genuine
   Being adult
   Speaking in my own vocabulary
   Being honest and open
   Stating my convictions while leaving freedom for theirs
   Boldly speaking out in radical situations
   Admitting I don't know all the answers
   Dealing with my own hang-ups first
3. Being Available
   Going to their events when adults are welcome
   Spending time with them and their friends
   Working and playing with them in various activities
   Taking kids to "away" games
   Picking up hitchhikers
   Inviting them to my home for dinner
   Initiating interviews
4. Showing Interest
   Remembering their names
   Learning about their world
   Being able to speak their language
   Listening to their music
   Adopting their symbols—beads, long hair, beard
   Finding areas where I can be of help
   Phone calls and letters re their accomplishments, interests

5. Communicating

  Talking to them every opportunity I get

  Slow, quiet listening; waiting for the chance to say some things

  Listening with the third ear for emotions

  One-to-one counseling

6. Leading

  Discovering and using their talents and interests

  Involving them in planning, decision-making, and executing activities

  Letting them find their own thing and do it

  Accepting their decisions

  Face them with the issues

  Holding unpopular positions which I think are best for them

  Giving them provocative, challenging books

  Offering them a host of options

  Presenting a better alternative by the way I live and act

  Getting them interested in trips, projects, studies to benefit them

  Creating celebrations and experiences for free expressions

  Getting them to camps, retreats

The second question of this group, "What are you doing to accomplish [your] purposes [with youth]?" revealed three new groups of skills:

7. Teaching

  Training others to reach out on a one-to-one basis

  Training leaders to program "exposure events"

  Reeducating adults to helping roles with youth

  Teaching the Scripture, presenting verbally and non-verbally the message of the love of Christ

  Teaching a class relating Bible, youth, and culture

  Personally confronting each youth with the claims of Christ

  Relating youth's ideas to Christian faith

8. Creating a Community

  Helping them to get to know each other

  Encouraging group awareness and sensitivity in everyday life

Finding Christ in each other, in everyone we encounter, in everything we do

Through involvement, make them aware of loneliness, deprivation, friendlessness

Helping forgiveness and acceptance to happen

Developing teamwork among youth in their activities

Trying to build a staff community

9. Encouraging Involvement

Involving kids where they can grow, experience, relate, share —volunteer work, seminars, schools, inner city, community

To Mexico yearly for service projects

Getting young people into the establishment

Creating opportunities for kids to think about, talk, act out their concerns

Discussing issues and trying to do something about them

The final question was, "If you were to describe the secret of your effectiveness, what are some of the ways of working with people that you have found effective?" It elicited no skills beyond those already revealed, but some new illustrations emerged for 8. Creating a Community: "developing groups who share at the deepest possible level" and "keeping the group open to friends of church youth."

Helping Youth into a Life of Faith

Research on Religious Development, a review of research literature on the religion of youth (1900-1969), established that adolescents who have direct personal experience of the presence of God differ from those who do not. Our study shows in what ways they differ: outlook on life, relations with people, motivation, and sense of moral responsibility. It demonstrates that relationships with God, man, and self are inextricably linked. This is why a personal faith is deemed important by those who have it; it is why a parent will ask, How do you help a son or daughter know a personal, caring God?

A fitting answer is given by leaders in Young Life, an international youth organization, who underscore the necessity of first taking the time to establish a relationship of love and trust. Once an open and cordial relationship is established, then questions of ultimate significance begin to surface.

"I don't know what I would do if God didn't exist. But does he?"

"Why doesn't he make it easier for us to believe?"

The Searching Questions

It is natural for the adolescent to feel that his faith depends upon himself, that he has to "make it" with God. And so he asks, Am I good enough?

Assuming the negative answer, he concludes that "God is not interested in me." Added to this concern is youth's fear of losing the respect of admired adults. Some are embarrassed to admit to parent or pastor that they struggle with doubts and question some things they have been taught.

Mingled with these feelings is the wistful, unvoiced question, "How do I 'get' faith?"

When the Bible is quoted, its words become enmeshed in the quicksand of further doubt. "The Bible was written for people centuries ago. By what stretch of imagination can I assume that it speaks to me? How do I know that interpretations I make (or you make) are correct ones?"

How can the words of Scripture ever be windows through which one sees an invisible God?

Finally, because youth respond as total persons, illness, depression, fatigue, or the pressure of circumstances tend to increase their feelings of religious uncertainty.

Times of Reflection and Decision

Youth retreats, informal discussions in a home, and personal conversations provide choice occasions for helping young people think into their relationship with God and voice both their lonesomeness for God and their desire to flee him.

At times like these, young people, preoccupied with standards of right and wrong, come to recognize an issue deeper than the matter of sins, per se. It is the question of authority: Do I remain the captain of my ship, or do I acknowledge the love and authority of the God who created me?

During times of reflection and decision, youth need the freedom to discuss the mystery of their rebellion and their proneness to go it alone. One can only encourage them to remain open to God's voice, allow times for listening, and take advantage of moments when he can be heard.

These are not times for a hard sell or for "thought-terminating cliches" which can force an artificial conversion that is mere acquiescence to a religious culture, without knowledge of the love and grace of God.

Youth need to understand that Christianity is a relationship with Christ, in which doubt is admissible because one relates to a person and not to a set of doctrines. Accepting a personal, caring God comes first; in coming to know him, one learns what is embodied in propositional truths.

When youth hear what God has done in the past and can do again for them, conversations about God become hope-inspiring occasions. Youth's attention shifts from themselves and their problems to the promises and possibilities of the Christian faith. The emptiness of a lonely life and the drawing power of love implicit in God's promise motivate them to enter God's possibilities as a child returns to his father's arms. In receiving a Savior, youth come to a personal transcendental experience with Jesus Christ.

A Supportive Congregation

A personal faith needs the sustaining power of a group. But what can give youth a sense of welcome and identification with his congregation?

Of the thirty-five possibilities tested, two were highly associated with positive, warm feelings toward one's congregation:

the first, to feel that one fits in well with some group in the congregation; and the second, to feel inspired at worship services.

It is hard to overemphasize the identification youth feel with their congregation when they are secure in a small group. If the youth interact first even in discussion groups of twelve to fifteen people, they later find the freedom to share themselves in the larger group.

An enigma for youth is why gatherings to celebrate their faith, such as Sunday morning worship, are often dull. Many find inspiration totally lacking in this function of their church family.

TABLE 12

Percentage Inspired by Local Worship Services
Ecumenical Sample
(N = 7,050)

	Percentage Saying Yes
A. Never inspired, only bored	11
B. No longer inspired, but I once was	11
C. Very often inspired	13
D. Quite often inspired	17
E. Sometimes inspired	32
F. Seldom inspired	15

Unlike adults, youth today are conscious not only of God's transcendence but also of his immanence. They look for more than a service that stresses his holiness, transcendence, and awesome greatness. They want more than the solemn beauty of a service where architecture, music, and liturgy create the sense of God's presence. Youth also want to worship the God who sits next to them in the fellowship of believers.

Youth want to worship a Christ, not only divine but also human, who is a part of rhythm, melody, and ordinary speech. They want a service that inspires, encourages, and helps them to feel what they are unable to make themselves feel.

One group of youth, after several weeks on the issue, agreed on three things they want in a morning worship service. First, it should be a time of singing, of expressing happiness over what God has done and is doing. If a service does not lift one's spirits, why speak of Good News?

Second, they want to learn something new and be stimulated intellectually by fresh insights into Christian truth.

Third, they want to participate and meet God in the presence of others. They want the service to impart a sense of warmth, love, and community.

A Stance toward Youth

Though this book is written for parents and youth leaders, it should not be assumed that adults have outgrown youth issues. On the contrary, the preceding analyses show how much adults are linked to youth needs.

Low self-esteem is probably passed on from parents.

Family disunity centers in parental conflict.

Social concern is characterized by youth's sharp criticism of congregational adults' lack of manifest caring.

Prejudice is found more readily among adults than among youth.

Loss of faith is an issue that is no respecter of age.

A ministry to youth is best seen as a collaborative effort—mutual seeking, helping, and working—in which adults freely admit their need to be helped in ways similar to youth. To believe that "no one has arrived" enables everyone, regardless of age or experience, to express the need for rebirth or renewal, for judgment and forgiveness.

The stance of common need reduces the age prejudice that characterizes most adults and mitigates the generational chauvinism of youth who feel superior to adults in such personal values as openness, honesty, and feeling for people.

It does not require that young people be seen as little adults. One can still view adolescents as possessors of special qualities—

liveliness, enthusiasm, honesty, idealism, and potential—and rightfully say, "I enjoy them," "They keep me young."

The preceding reflections draw attention to at least two imperatives in a youth ministry—*mutuality* and *mission*. Youth of all subcultures want the warmth of an accepting group which is *mutuality*. They need activities which give them a sense of purpose; that is *mission*. Within these two polarities, there is powerful need for *educational experiences* for youth and adults that open minds, develop skills, clarify values, and encourage commitment.

Leadership Training:
A Case History

Michael Warren

The following account of a leadership training program might at
first seem dated, especially since it was developed ten years ago.
Yet it is presented here because the writer/editor judges it to
have validity for contemporary ministry to youth. It remains a
concrete model of leadership development that could be adapted
to many contemporary contexts, such as the development of
leadership within a particular high school or among student leaders of several different schools in the same area, the development of peer ministers within one or among a cluster of parishes,
the preparation of leaders for summer programs of volunteer service, or the preparation of youth teams for Christian Experience
Weekends.

Possibly the most exciting aspect of contemporary youth ministry is the degree to which young people who have been ministered to have come forward and asked to be allowed themselves
to exercise a ministry to either their peers or to younger
teens. Leadership development is becoming more and more of an
issue among adult leaders in youth ministry and among young
people themselves. Nor is it surprising that young people, who
can vote at eighteen and who in their mid-teens show considerable expertise in science or the arts, are coming forward for a
true participative role in ministry. At the present time, however,
relatively little has been written about some of the exciting work
being done to develop leadership and ministry among young people themselves. The following report of the Xaverian Leadership
Institute, dated though it may be, is offered with the modest

hope of encouraging others to write of their efforts in this area of leadership development.

──────────────── ▲ ────────────────

In 1966 a group of four teachers from four different Catholic high schools operated by the Xaverian Brothers met about a dozen times to plan and eventually launch a venture to develop leadership among the students of their schools elected to their Student Activity Councils. All four Brothers had in one way or other experimented with approaches to leadership development within their own individual schools. They had come together out of a need to collaborate with others with a similar vision of the importance of nurturing the leadership potential of young people.

Early in their meetings they agreed on the purpose of their proposed program and the premises behind it. These premises were the following:

1. If we bring together students of already proven leadership ability and foster interaction among them, they will learn much about leadership from each other.

2. If we bring together leaders in student activities from different schools and let them share ideas on their student activity programs, the programs in all schools should improve.

3. If we bring together students who are Christians and give them opportunities to express their faith, the result will be an intense experience of unity as a Christian community and a consequent strengthening of faith.

These basic principles, once agreed upon, gave some direction to later planning. They proved to be quite sound as guiding principles for the Xaverian Leadership Institute (XLI), as the program they developed eventually came to be known. The precise type of program used to implement these principles, however, was more difficult to decide on. Basically, the group had two models to choose from. The first was the model of instruction and learning-by-listening, which would have set up the program as a series of classes and seminars on leadership problems and skills, especially those skills and problems related to schools. The second model was that of interaction and learning-by-doing. In this plan, the group of program participants would be broken into four sub-groups or councils. The councils would then have to elect officers and perform a series of tasks much as a Student Activity Council does in a high school. Such a plan would encourage leadership to grow within each council and emerge in the larger group. It would foster an experience of leadership-in-action. This second, more participative model was the one adopted for the XLI.

The description of the actual running of the Xaverian Leadership Institute might be best presented in a present-tense examination of three aspects of the program: the function of the staff, the role of the student groups, and the schedule. The staff of the program could be divided into two groups, the program directors and the council moderators. The program directors number five, the director and his four assistants. Their role in the XLI is very limited, subtle, but important. The director, for example, gives no talks during the Institute, except for a very brief welcome at the beginning and a report of his impressions of the program at the very end. He rather tries to be aware of the overall tone of the program by quietly sitting in on various group meetings. He also takes care of any administrative business that comes up during the program.

His four assistants function quite similarly, except that they give the only formal talks presented during the program. Each morning they meet with a different council and present the talk they have prepared, answering any questions that result. Thus each Assistant Director gives the same talk four times in the course of the Institute. The titles of these talks are "Group Dynamics in the Student Council," "Aims and Objectives of the Student Council," "Self-Concept and Leadership," and "20th Century Christian Leadership." The importance of these talks does not lie in their content so much as in the contact of the students with adults who encourage them to take a more positive view of their own leadership ability. All five directors meet frequently with the executive council, described below.

In a sense, the council moderators have a far more important role in the XLI than do the directors. Each of the four young adults who function as council moderators is the advisor to a different council made up of twenty students. Though he lives and works with his group continually during the four days, he does not directly "lead" his group; an elected council president has that function. Somewhat like a Student Activity Council moderator in a high school, the council moderator is more a resource person. When called upon by the group, he advises, bringing to discussions a more mature viewpoint, encouraging the group to take upon itself as many leadership responsibilities as possible. It is interesting that at all XLI programs the youngsters recognized and keenly appreciated the subtle and quietly effective leadership provided by these council moderators.

By far, the most important role at the XLI is that of the student groups themselves. For the program to succeed, each of these four groups or councils must quickly elect its own officers, establish a group identity, set up committees to accomplish group tasks, and get involved in competing with the other student councils. The tasks given them at the opening of the program are devised to help the councils accomplish just these goals. In fact, the bulk of the program of the XLI involves the carrying out of these tasks, which are of two types: those that are to be carried out by each council as a separate group of twenty, and those that are to be accomplished by committees made up of members drawn from each council.

The first task for the councils is the election of their own officers and the selection of a council name, council cheer, and council song. At the same time they must select representatives for the nine inter-council committees described below. Next, each council must plan a presentation at the Council Fire the second evening of the program. Thirdly, the third evening each council must put on a talent show. Finally, each group is presented with a council problem to which they must come with a solution to be acted out in a skit the final night of the Institute. These council problems are descriptions of very human problem situations that can arise in the running of a Student Activity Council. All these activities—the Council Fire presentation, the talent show, and the problem dramatization must somehow actively involve all twenty council members.

The second category of tasks, which might be called inter-council activities, involve the boys with one another across council lines. These committees and their functions could be listed thus (asterisks indicate that the committees must publish a program of events):

WORKSHOP COMMITTEES AND PROCEDURE

Advisory Committee

Members: President and Secretary and committee chairman of each council

Function: To consult daily with members of the staff

Sports Committee

Members: Approximately three members from each student council

Function: To assist in the planning and operation of the afternoon sports and recreation program*

Talent Show Committee

Members: Approximately two members from each student council

Function: Assist the director of the talent show in planning and presentation* (Join Banquet Committee after talent show)

Problem Skits Committee

Members: Approximately two members from each student council

Function: To assist in the planning and operation of the problem skits*

Campfire-Art Committee

Members: Approximately three members from each student council

Function: 1. To plan and carry out the operation of the evening campfire program*

2. Plan and execute a graphic representation of each council

Workshop Report Committee

Members: Approximately three members from each student council, one of whom should be the secretary. Those with typing proficiency preferred.

Function: To compile and produce the workshop booklet to be presented to each participant on the final day.

Banquet Committee

Members: Approximately three members from each student council

Function: To make the arrangements for set-up, decorations, etc.* of the Banquet on the final evening

Workshop Highlights Committee

Members: Approximately three members from each student council

Function: To publish a Daily Summary of Events - newspaper style

Liturgical Committee

Members: One member from each student council
Function: To prepare and plan all liturgical services

From the above description of the tasks assigned the participants at XLI several things will be clear. First, the youngsters are expected to accomplish a great deal within four days. The program is indeed an exhausting one for the students though it is rather relaxing for the directors. Secondly, the boys must develop quickly a spirit of cooperation and competition. This means that they are under great pressure to learn how to work with one another and how to contribute one's talents to a group effort while maintaining one's own creativity and individuality. Under this pressure many little human problems and crises develop and are profitably worked through.

Thirdly, once the whole operation gets into high gear, it can all become quite complex. At times the boys become so intent on accomplishing tasks and meeting deadlines that there is a rush of mad, scurrying, hectic activity. The organization needed to coordinate all this activity is supplied by the advisory committee, composed of the program directors, the council presidents and secretaries, and the chairmen of the eight work committees, a total of twenty-one persons. The meetings of this giant committee-for-committees, though rather informal, serves to keep every council and every committee in touch with the activities of all other groups, as well as in touch with the tone of the whole program. These meetings also keep the intense competition which develops in balanced perspective.

Possibly the best way of presenting the schedule is to outline the actual one followed at the most recent XLI and then make some clarifying comments. The schedule is as follows:

ACTIVITY CALENDAR

TUESDAY - AUGUST 27

4:00 p.m. - 6:00 p.m.	Registration
5:00 p.m. - 6:00 p.m.	Staff meeting
6:00 p.m.	Supper
7:30 p.m.	General Assembly (Keynote address) Christian Leadership & Theme "Are You the One" - Headmaster, Brother Richard Kerressey, CFX, St. John's Prep
8:30 p.m. - 9:00 p.m.	Council meetings a. introduce council members to each other and to council moderator b. find song, name, cheer for council by Thursday evening c. decide how council will pray together
9:00 p.m. - 10:30 p.m.	Social hour
10:30 p.m.	Assembly - rules - regulations
11:00 p.m.	Community service
12:00 p.m.	Lights out

WEDNESDAY - AUGUST 28

7:30 a.m.	Rise
8:00 a.m.	Breakfast
9:00 a.m.	Assembly
	a. announcements
	b. committee workshops - assigned
	c. introduce council problem
9:30 a.m. - 11:30 a.m.	Council meeting
	a. talk by one of the assistant directors followed by discussion
	b. election of officers
	c. appointment of representatives to committees
12:00	Community worship
12:45 p.m. - 1:30 p.m.	Lunch
1:30 p.m.	Meeting of new officers
1:45 p.m. - 2:30 p.m.	Workshop committees
2:50 p.m.	Assembly - installation of officers
3:30 p.m. - 5:00 p.m.	Recreation (sports)
6:00 p.m.	Supper
7:00 p.m. - 8:30 p.m.	Swap shop
8:30 p.m.	Movie
10:30 p.m.	Cokes
12:00 p.m.	Lights out

THURSDAY - AUGUST 29

7:00 a.m.	Rise
8:00 a.m.	Breakfast
9:00 a.m. - 9:30 a.m.	Speaker - Discussion

10:00 a.m. - 11:45 a.m.	Council meeting
12:00 n. - 1:00 p.m.	Lunch
1:30 p.m. - 2:15 p.m.	Council meeting - Business
2:30 p.m. - 3:15 p.m.	Workshop committee
3:15 p.m. - 3:30 p.m.	Assembly
3:30 p.m. - 4:30 p.m.	Recreation
5:00 p.m.	Community worship
6:00 p.m.	Cook-out and Camp Fire Program Council, cheers and songs
10:30 p.m.	Evening prayer (accompanied by song) (Liturgical committee)
12:00 p.m.	Lights out

FRIDAY - AUGUST 30

7:00 a.m.	Rise
8:00 a.m.	Breakfast
9:00 a.m. - 11:30 a.m.	Speaker and council meeting
12:00 n. - 1:00 p.m.	Lunch
1:15 p.m. - 2:00 p.m.	Workshop committees
2:00 p.m. - 2:50 p.m.	Swap shop
3:00 p.m. - 5:00 p.m.	Recreation - Rehearsal for talent show
5:00 p.m.	Community worship
6:00 p.m.	Supper
7:30 p.m. - 8:15 p.m.	Council problem - (practice) skit
8:30 p.m. - 10:30 p.m.	Talent Show - Pizza and cokes

SATURDAY - AUGUST 31

8:00 a.m.	Rise
8:30 a.m.	Breakfast
9:00 a.m. - 10:10 a.m.	Speaker - Discussion
10:20 a.m. - 11:30 a.m.	Council meeting (business)
12:00 n.	Lunch - Picnic
1:15 p.m. - 2:15 p.m.	Swap shop
2:30 p.m. - 3:30 p.m.	Rehearsal for skits
3:30 p.m. - 4:30 p.m.	Workshop committees
4:30 p.m. - 5:30 p.m.	Recreation or continue above
6:00 p.m.	Eucharistic banquet - Council banquet
8:30 p.m.	Problem skits
9:30 p.m.	Movie
11:30 p.m.	Lights out

SUNDAY - SEPTEMBER 1

7:50 a.m.	Rise
8:20 a.m.	Breakfast
8:30 a.m. - 9:10 a.m.	Council meeting (evaluation of program)
9:15 a.m. - 9:45 a.m.	Assembly
10:00 a.m.	Mass - Departure

An item on the schedule that needs special explanation is
the swap shop, which is a meeting according to either school size
or to student activities for the purpose of exchanging ideas on the

running of student activity programs in our schools. For example, in one swap shop the boys meet according to the size of their school enrollment. Thus, those from the largest schools meet to discuss their problems while those from the intermediate size and smaller schools form their own groups. In another swap shop the boys meet according to the different student activities they are interested in: social, athletic, cultural, or religious. In general, the swap shop provides a valuable forum for exchanging ideas on the running of a student council.

Another important comment on the schedule: it is entirely functional. There were many adaptations made in it in the course of the Institute, mostly on the suggestions offered by the Advisory Committee. Moreover, there is a general evaluation of the schedule on the final morning of the program when many suggestions for future schedules are made. Most recently, for instance, the boys agreed that we should drop the films as being unnecessary distractions from the more important work of the program.

Finally, mention should be made of the banquet which, together with the problem skits, forms the high point of the Xaverian Leadership Institute. The banquet takes place in two steps: the Eucharistic banquet, followed by another meal done in somewhat sumptuous "neo-Klondike" banquet style, with the dining hall decorated and arranged so as to resemble a real banquet hall (no small feat in a summer camp setting). The meal itself is an elaborate, multi-course dinner. In any other context such a banquet could easily become mock heroic with its combination of splendid food in entirely less-than-splendid surroundings, but the many incongruities are ignored by the teenagers in their exuberance at having accomplished so much in so few days.

Any account of the XLI would be incomplete without some description of the dimension of faith that sets so much of its tone. It is remarkable that each time we have run the program, many boys have claimed that the experience was more meaningful in terms of religious experience than the retreats many of them had participated in as high school juniors. The specific aspects of the program that contribute to this spirit of faith are difficult to determine. There are no spiritual talks given in the program; even at Mass the homilies are dialogue homilies moderated by the celebrant. There is general agreement among the directors, however, that it is the celebration of the liturgy which more than anything else contributes to the intense experience of Christian community. Planned by the councils, the daily Mass liturgy is carried out with a spirit of participation few of the students have experienced in their parish life. Though attendance at the Eucharist was voluntary, it became clearly the high point of the day, especially of the final three days of the Institute.

The presence of two excellent chaplains experienced in working with young people also added to the Christian tone of the program. Their experience and their understanding of the problems of teenagers gave them a rapport with the boys that issued in many confessions and many private conferences. No doubt much religious confusion was dispelled in these conferences which at times ran into the wee hours. If modern theology sees the role of the priest as one of bringing people together to realize their union in Christ, these two priests are fine exemplars of that role.

Apart from the above factual description of the Xaverian Leadership Institute, the writer can make only modest claims for this program, which filled a need at a particular time and in a special setting. Nevertheless the contemporary need for innovative programs for developing youth leadership calls for others to develop similar programs suited to different groups and settings. Such efforts in turn will need very few claims made for them. The attempt itself tends to become self-justifying and mutually enriching for all involved.

Adolescent Girls:
A Two-Year Study

Gisela Konopka

One of the needs often voiced by those active in youth ministry is the need for good research on the attitudes and needs of young people. Many are already aware of the value of Merton Strommen's recent research on the attitudes of youth. Less well-publicized but equally valuable is the research of Gisela Konopka, Director of the Center for Youth Development and Research at the University of Minnesota. Dr. Konopka's work has the special value of having focused exclusively on teenage girls. Although there is less and less segregation by sex in Catholic ministry to youth, focus on the specific attitudes and needs of girls will enrich all those eager to grow in their understanding of young people.

Supported by a grant from the Lilly Endowment, Inc., Dr. Konopka and a staff of specially trained researchers in twelve different states undertook to identify the wide variety of needs, aspirations and concerns of young women twelve to eighteen years old. The 920 women, interviewed in both rural and urban settings, represented every racial, religious and ethnic group and a range of socio-economic backgrounds. One-third of the women were adjudicated delinquent, one-third were active in youth organizations, and one-third fell into neither category. An informally structured but open-ended 60-90 minute interview with each girl was taped. Subsequently, these sessions were analyzed according to the girl's views, beliefs, and feelings on: education, careers, marriage, children, the women's movement, adults, friends, drugs and alcohol, sexuality, social and political concerns, relationships with adults, experiences with and recommendations for youth organizations.

Dr. Konopka's book containing her findings and recommendations based on them has been published by Prentice-Hall under the title *Young Girls: A Portrait of Adolescence*. Poems by the girls quoted in the following presentation are taken from this book. The following article and interview are both from the Fall 1975 issue of *Center Quarterly Focus*, the publication of the Center for Youth Development and Research, University of Minnesota, St. Paul, Minn. 55108. They are included here in a section on the development of leadership particularly because of Dr. Konopka's several references to the functions of service organizations dealing with youth.   *Michael Warren*

▲

I have always maintained that when we set out to talk about people we should first let *them* talk about themselves. I cannot bring 920 girls here to speak to you in person, but I can let a few speak through their poetry. They write beautiful poetry. This poem was written by a 15-year-old girl in a delinquency institution. She talks about herself and her generation:

I am a bottle
sealed with feeling
too deep for anyone else.
I am a bottle
floating in an eternal ocean of people
trying to help.
I am a bottle
keeping my fragile content inside it,
always afraid of breaking and exposing me.
I am a bottle
frail and afraid of the rock and afraid of the storm,
for if the storm or rocks burst or crack me
I sink and become part of the ocean.
I am a person, I am a person
in the people of the world.

Though I have to generalize about what we found in our study, it is important to remember that *every person is somewhat different from any other.* I also want to say at the outset that I am talking about reality—what we actually heard, not necessarily what we wished to hear. This poem by a 16-year-old speaks to individuality:

I used to be a grape in a bunch
and all the other grapes were the same.
But now I am an apple, crisp and fresh
and everyone is different.
My, how life has changed.

These 12- to 18-year-olds were born into national and international strife with the beginning of inflation and depression. The general environment of their parent generation was characterized by prosperity, though it does not follow that all of them participated in prosperity. Their grandparents lived through the depression of the 30's. Each generation grows up in a different kind of context. The girls we interviewed hold high hopes of better justice for all. Their generation comes after the fighting generation, and they are experiencing the harsh reaction against the preceding rebellion. They are very self-conscious adolescents, even more so because they are female. Though we rarely heard the girls talk abstractly about their self concepts, everything they said was permeated by their concept of self.

I shall try to report what they said according to what I thought was significant to them: (1) their present drives, their dreams for the future; (2) their family, important as a supporting and limiting power; (3) their friends, important as mirrors of themselves; (4) the organizations they joined; (5) the school, again important as a supporting and limiting power; and (6) the political and social scene.

I
LIFE GOALS

Marriage

This generation of young women wants both marriage and a career. They have thought it through in rather a calm way. In general they do not expect to marry early. "I want to get married when the time comes and the time is right. I don't want to rush it because I want to make sure. It's like if there was a problem you have to pay so much money to get a divorce and I don't think it's right. If two people love each other they should be able to stay together without those laws between them." I'm not saying there will be no teenage marriages, but on the average they think after 22 is a good time to get married. One thing stands out: marriage means a great deal to them but they do not want to be married to a domineering male. Again there are exceptions, but this is feared with great realism, particularly in the poverty area. "I would rather be more like friends with my husband. That comes first." "I just want to marry someone who shares a lot of the same interests I do and we can get along with each other."

Children

Many girls want children, but they know they have a choice as to when and how many. Most of them wanted three; many wanted fewer; very few wanted more. They thought of raising children mostly in terms of very young children. This business of really raising a human being had not sunk in very deeply.

Divorce

We found an extraordinary fear of divorce. When they talked freely this terrible fear came through. Typical statements: "What is the use of getting married if you just get divorced?" "The children will be hurt."

Careers

The choice of careers is influenced by life experiences—by what we might call adult models. Organizations and schools have given them very little conscious exposure to such models. Counselors in schools seemed to be especially ineffective. "Talking to them is like talking to a brick wall." White collar jobs are preferred. The most tradition-bound group were the adjudicated girls.

II
SEX

Sex is talked about very calmly by most of the girls. They accept themselves as sexual beings. This is not to say they all wanted to have premarital sex, but practically all of them were very tolerant of others who do. Even if they said, "That's not for me," they were tolerant. "I want to wait until I get married, but I don't look down on a friend."

There was enormous fear, however, of being used sexually. They believed a boyfriend should be an equal, a friend, "gentle, nice, someone who listens." *Listens* was written large. Practically none of the girls would want to just go from one love affair to another.

Sexual Abuse and Incest

We found that first sex experiences which had been disastrous and harmful usually happened to girls in their own homes. I'm not talking exclusively of incest. Sometimes it was the father, of course, but often it was a brother, another relative, or the mother's boyfriend. The tragedy is that these girls, when they run away from an intolerable situation, are treated as offenders, not as victims. We do exactly the most harmful thing in such a situation: we put them into institutions where they are separated completely from men and cannot learn any healthy relationship to the other sex. Furthermore, they are labeled. As one of the girls said, "Well, if they put me there, I am bad." This increases their sense of inferiority. They become outcasts.

Pregnancy before Marriage

The attitude of most of the girls toward pregnancy before marriage again is one of tolerance. This is not a militant generation. Many would want to keep the child, but tend to think of the child only as a baby. Some talk about adoption. They discuss abortion openly. About half of the group were strongly for abortion, half were strongly against it.

Sex information was incredibly poor—an absolute disgrace in 1975. To be sure, there were exceptions. One girl said, "When I first found out I was pregnant I didn't even know what pregnant meant and I went to the nurse and she told me 'that means you're going to have a little baby,' and I said 'What?' And then I told my parents and then I thought I had really been bad." Many did not even know about menstruation.

To summarize, I don't think we found a sex revolution, but there is greater tolerance for premarital sex. There is still an enormous need to help people understand sex. The institutionalized girl was the worst off. She had gone through horrible experiences and most of the time was a victim. She was treated as the offender and made to feel an outcast.

III
RELATIONSHIP TO ADULTS

Generation Gap

I would like to discuss the relationship of the girls to adults in terms of three myths that we must destroy. One is the much publicized generation gap. Naturally there is always a generation difference, but I would not say it is a great gap. The values the girls hold are often quite similar to those of the adult world. What they expect of people is what we expect of people, too. Negative qualities of adults they mentioned were "phony, nosey, grouchy, greedy, self-conscious; they stereotype us, they don't like us." Positives named included "fun to be with, understanding, respect us, will listen, care, trust us and deserve trust, are patient, fair and just."

Relationship to Parents

The second myth is that the family is totally falling apart, that young people want to get out of the family. We found they want a family very badly, yearn for a family if they don't have it. A girl who was thrown out by her family said in a poem: "Loneliness is missing your family, it's not knowing what to say."

Really surprising to us was that the most significant adult named by a majority of the girls was mother. They want to be related to mother and often have very good relationships with their mother. "She is just fantastic. She can yell at us, but we really respect her. She is always there to help. She understands, she works, and she knows who she is." That last sentence was rather typical. The nonsense about the working mother being the worst is not true. I think young people are quite realistic about parents.

Next in rank among significant adults was father. Yet he showed up as more authoritarian, often less communicative, and tending to lose contact when the girls reach adolescence. Fathers, it was reported, don't want daughters to grow up; they want them to remain their little girl. "Oh, he's quite tolerant about a lot of things, but, oh boy, if I go out, oh my little girl, that shouldn't happen."

Another finding, not startling but exciting, was the warm relationship with the grandparent generation. These are real people whom the girls love. This is also true of uncles and aunts. "I can talk with them. My grandmother tells me she wasn't always good, but my mother would never say that."

Permissiveness

The third myth I want to hit hard is that this is a permissive society. We found incredibly authoritarian families, the vast majority in fact. We found the battered adolescent. "When I do something wrong he beats the shit out of me. If I wouldn't clean the table right, or especially if I talked back, or if I started to cry or showed any feeling, my stepfather would beat me up." Or, "She wouldn't let me go nowhere. She beat me with braided ropes, extension cords, yardsticks, boards, whatever she could find when she was mad." A girl described being brought in by police for something she had done. The parents turned to the policeman and said, "What would you do?" He said, "Well, if she were my girl I'd give her a good beating with a police belt." "All right," the father said, "give me the belt" (it has a big buckle) and in front of everybody the girl is beaten with the belt. She gets hysterical, falls on the floor, starts laughing and laughing. The more she laughs the more they beat her. Then she walks upstairs and vomits all day. Again, as with sex offenses, these girls are not treated as victims, always as offenders. With some exceptions, the treatment in delinquency institutions is abominable. Too much still is done to degrade the girls. One girl said, "My mother always told me, 'Whenever you see anyone crying, just try to talk to them.' But up here you can't do it because they will start yelling at you, 'You shut your mouth or you will get three days strict you know.' Being locked up, that's the worst. You can't get out, you can't say what you want, you can't do what you want. They bust teenagers for just anything. There is nothing you can do. They're just over you." The hate such conditions create is illustrated by one girl's solution: "Blow everybody up and get people to know what they are doing." Some institutions do try to provide help, especially those that are smaller. Quoting another interviewee: "Our counselor here will try to help you. If you don't want to go to her you can talk to one of the girls."

IV
PEERS

Another important subject we explored was how adolescent girls feel about their peers. What about the loneliness that showed up so strongly in my previous study, *The Adolescent Girl in Conflict* (Prentice-Hall, 1966)? It is still there. Friends of their own age are very important, but adults are just as important. The girls stressed that friends must be trustworthy and you must be able to talk to them. That goes for both boys and girls, not just girls. What they do when they are with friends is pretty much the same, whether the group includes boys or not. Some have sex relations, but they want the boy also as a *friend*. The delinquent girls talked a great deal about how their boyfriends support them, give them some sense of value. This prop is taken away the moment they are placed in an institution. These girls also suffer from distrust by the community. One interviewee who had become pregnant before marriage was not allowed to go to the same school she had attended, a youth organization of which she was a member immediately excluded her, the parents of her friends did not allow their daughters to communicate with her, and she became a total isolate. This kind of thing we heard frequently.

We found few gang activities. Where they existed, girls were part of the gang, not just the auxiliary. Though there was violence in the gangs and they retaliated with violence, most girls disliked the violence.

Suicide attempts were frequent in our survey population. The reasons are the same as those found in any other population. Enormous loneliness, which we find again among the aged, is one. I was interested in a couplet quoted to us by girls across the country:

Loneliness is a silent jail
Without cellmates, parole or bail.

Other reasons for suicide attempts were severe conflicts, either with the boyfriend or with the parents. Occasionally they were related to depressive drugs, especially alcohol. I am often asked if we found much homosexuality or lesbianism. The answer is we didn't. We certainly found it in the delinquency institutions, but all of us know it flourishes there because of the total segregation from boys. Oddly enough, in terms of attitudes, homosexuality was the most disliked quality. Tolerance about sex did not seem to extend to homosexuality or lesbianism.

V
DRUGS AND ALCOHOL

Not surprisingly, we found an increase in alcohol use, partially because there is less conflict with society about it and partially because it is often fostered by the parents. The girls themselves stressed the negative effects of hard drugs. They see them as a danger, but as for marijuana—most of them hardly consider it a drug. They want it to be legalized. Half of the girls said they do not use drugs but they all knew of them. That applies just as much to rural areas as to urban areas. A question we asked was: "Why do you think girls take drugs? Is it different from why boys take drugs?" They said no, it was kind of the same: curiosity, peer pressure, finding drugs agreeable. But they thought boys also take drugs to prove their masculinity. Whether they evaluated the boys correctly I don't know.

We thought drug information often increased curiosity, but on the other hand it showed quite well the different effects drug use can have. We felt that strong motivation is required to stop taking drugs. "My boyfriend doesn't want me to take drugs and I want to please him." Or "I want to have healthy children, so that's why I stopped." They feel they cannot talk to adults about drugs. Most of them thought their parents did not know it when they took drugs. Among girls who belonged to youth organizations (one-third of our sample) most knew about or had taken drugs, but they said, "Oh my goodness, we would never mention it there!"

VI
SOCIAL AND POLITICAL INVOLVEMENT

My first impression when I looked at this part of the material was: this is really catastrophic! They are terribly self-concerned, they don't know how to participate in the political scene, they are disenchanted about things political, they don't feel responsible as citizens. After more careful reading of the material and discussion with my researchers, I recognized that first of all we must think of adolescence as a period of basic self-concern anyhow. Second, many adults do not participate in the political scene either. We were interviewing at the height of Watergate, so that had a strong influence. Finally, we have to remember that the girls actually were very concerned about issues but they did not know how to translate their concern into action. This was the first time they had been asked what their thoughts were. They talked about war, about government cheating, about race relations, and about issues relating to youth—e.g., the draft and the juvenile court. We also talked with them about the women's movement. Very often they saw only the extremes in the movement, which they didn't care for. But when we probed a little deeper we saw that they have simply accepted as their due what others fought for: equal pay for equal work, open opportunities for women, etc. So although they are not revolutionaries, they are involved, as this poem illustrates. It was written by a 16-year-old who has dropped out of school but wants very much to be a lawyer.

You talk about the problems of the world
And I am not allowed to speak because I am just a little
    girl.
But there is something I would like to say to you, you know
It's my world too.
You think that you can understand more than anyone at all
But mister, you are really short when you think you are tall.
And I'm not allowed to give my opinions because I'm not as
    big as you.
Try not to forget
It's my world too.
They talk about young people all the time
But they don't think of others who are out of line
And some problems mean nothing to you
But while I am living here

It's my world too.
What I want is the best for everyone
Cuz thinking of yourself is not good in a long run.
So think about what you want for me and you
And while you are thinking, remember
It's my world too.

VII
SCHOOL

School was often seen as very positive, mostly because the girls find friends there. Race discrimination hurts deeply, especially when teachers insult minority girls or show fear of them. Their anger at being treated differently flares out. "What do they think I am, an animal?" Many girls experience enjoyment in school. When we asked what they expect of school they spoke of friendship and understanding, but also of learning. Often the subjects they preferred were those we consider difficult. Exceptions were the delinquent girls who usually have been treated abominably and feel that school has nothing for them.

VIII
YOUTH ORGANIZATIONS

We found it rather sad that youth organizations seem to have little meaning to the girls. In general they found them childish. Perhaps the most serious finding was an indirect one: when we asked them about significant adults, two girls out of 920 named two people from youth serving organizations. The girls do not think they can talk with youth workers if they have problems. "Organizations are only for the good ones."

I read an article recently stating that nobody knows what kind of people we want to develop. If we don't know that, then I think we should really give up. Every society has to decide what kind of people it wants. To my thinking it is really quite simple. I go to the ideals of the Bill of Rights, which I did not invent: (1)

an open free society based on the proposition that the purpose of government is to advance and protect human rights; (2) a representative form of democratic government which means that citizens must be encouraged to participate in their own fate and have the necessary knowledge to do so, otherwise it will not survive; (3) a society ruled by law; (4) an egalitarian non-discriminatory society with equal opportunity for everybody; (5) a pluralistic society with opportunity for groups to have a variety of life styles without harming others or feeling that one or the other style is inferior. If we combine these ideals we get a sense of direction, a sense of how to deal with our youth in the family, in schools, in youth organizations and in corrections. The time has passed for rigid, laid-out programs for young people. Most significant are the *people* who work with them. They not only must understand these youngsters but must consciously see how they themselves relate to people. They must be able to listen to and respect young people and permit their genuine participation. I felt very strongly that these young girls were asking us not only to listen to them but to convey something of the meaning of life to them. They want to talk, they want to think things through, they want absolute honesty.

The young people we talked to were very sober. We must help them feel that there is hope, that there is compassion, that joy and commitment actually are possible. So I will end with a thought from Morris West who understands the stark reality of life but also understands its beauty:

> To reject the joy of living is to insult Him who provides it,
> And who gave us the gift of laughter along with the gift of
> tears.

Our young population has that gift. We squelch it far too often; we do not enhance it enough.

INTERVIEW WITH DR. KONOPKA

Dogma and Direction

Q. How do we move between the two extremes of trying to impose ideals upon young people (making them what we think they should be) and not giving them any direction at all?

G.K. This seems to me to be one of the philosophic questions that I hope everybody can go back and discuss with the girls themselves. To think through the difference between dogma and direction is an exciting experience at almost any age. I don't expect we will ever find the complete answer. But if our ideal is a population capable of making choices on two grounds (1) consideration of other people and (2) facts, then we have to learn to look at facts, to assess them, and to develop a measuring stick for making choices. I think we can help people learn how to make choices without imposing our own styles on them. We must allow them a large number of alternatives.

Building Trust

Q. In what ways can a worker cooperatively build trust between group and leader?

G.K. First of all, you surely don't build trust with gimmicks. Kids very quickly spot phoniness. I don't learn trust in a weekend therapy session, by falling back blindfolded and being caught before I drop. Since the whole "bag" at that moment is to create trust, I assume they won't let me drop. Does that mean I can trust the next guy I meet in the community who wants to cut my throat if I disagree with him? No.

Another way some of us try to build trust is by sitting across the desk from a person saying, "You know I understand who you are and what you think, and you must trust me." It doesn't work. Trust is built slowly, through experience. When you are working with people, be honest. By that I don't mean be brutal. But be open; don't pretend the world is all good when you know it is not. When they need you, be available. It takes time to build trust.

If you are asking me how to build trust with very distrustful young people I would need an hour to discuss it. You have to undo so much. But it is not as difficult as most adults seem to think. What came out over and over in our study was this incredible yearning to have somebody to talk to.

Meeting Needs—Toward Greater Effectiveness

Q. Should every girls' organization try to meet all the needs of all girls, or are there some basic needs or concerns that all organizations should broaden their base to meet?

G.K. In my opinion no organization and no individual can ever serve all the needs of all the people. That's impossible. So it's all right sometimes to say we will just cut out a certain slice from the whole pie and, let's say, provide services for a particular neighborhood, or serve girls in a particular area of interest. What I think is dangerous, though, is separation on the basis of delinquency or race or ethnic background.

Now, are there basic needs all organizations should meet? I think so. We may not always agree on all needs and concerns but we have to know them and develop our thinking and our programs around them, based on some philosophy. I talked about this in the *Bill of Rights* context. For instance, if we believe people must be able to make choices, otherwise our democracy will die, then it behooves all organizations to provide experience in making choices rather than having authoritarian leaders who set the program and expect everyone to work by the book.

If we agree that self-esteem is the basis for respecting other people, then we have to provide the ingredients which enhance self-esteem: real participation in decision-making, for instance, not just asking for opinions; genuine acceptance of young people as equals, not just as pre-adults. We can translate almost every one of these basic "shoulds" or ideals, combine them with what we understand, and make them part of our programs.

So, I would say all youth organizations have to fulfill some of the basic needs of human beings and serve a wide variety of young people, yet they cannot reach all of them.

Q. You mentioned earlier that the girls had quit some of the organizations when they were in junior high school. Can you elaborate on that—what they liked about some organizations and disliked about others?

G.K. Okay, what do they like? Written very big is opportunity for adventure—the real possibility to get out and do things that are different, not the tame camping or the usual kind of summer program. I don't mean necessarily running the rapids but just going somewhere else, meeting totally different people, discussing new and exciting things. Wish for excitement is very big in that age range.

I don't usually name names, but 4-H got a good press so I'll use it as a concrete example. One thing the girls liked there was the coed organization which allowed them to be with boys at some times. We found kind of a general feeling: "No, we don't want always to be with boys but we like to have the opportunity to work with them and not just to party with them." Second, they liked individualized projects—not programs where everybody has to do the same thing. They liked the feeling of doing something distinct and getting recognition for it. Third, they liked being allowed to travel. "It wasn't just going on a vacation. We did something, we exhibited something, we worked on something together, and we were somewhere else." Being involved in actual helping also is important to them, as is the kind of adult they meet. Their most negative reaction is to the adult who treats them like little kids and looks down on them.

I think all organizations could be more effective. One of my great hopes is that we will get away from the notion of compartmentalization—school is for learning, youth organizations are for fun, parents are for nurture. We have to work together and eliminate the jealousies among us. For that we need the right kind of people. Partially they have to be found, but partially they can also be developed through training. At the Center we are starting a two-year project, funded by the Lilly Endowment, Incorporated, in which we hope to train 400 significant personnel within eight youth-serving organizations plus some staff from corrections.

Reaching Troubled Adolescents

Q. Do you have any ideas on how organizations and resources can better reach troubled adolescents?

G.K. First of all, do not segregate them. Why do we call one "troubled" and another "untroubled?" I have not yet seen an adolescent who is not troubled at times. In fact, I have not seen a person who is not troubled at times, regardless of age, but in adolescence everything is worse. It's a more touchy age. Almost every experience is brand new. The ability to see failure in perspective has not yet been developed. For instance, you have fallen in love and the boy leaves you. You haven't experienced this before and you are ready to commit suicide. In contrast, I feel scared before I give a speech but I have experienced over and over that somehow it will work out. So I am anxious, but not desperate.

My answer then is: first, don't segregate; second, take the troubles seriously, but don't look on the "troubled" as a group apart; third, understand the enormous range of normalcy. In general, much of what we consider emotionally disturbed is normal.

Q. What are the alternatives to traditional ways of dealing with runaways?

G.K. Certainly they vary. Sometimes we treat runaways as offenders rather than as victims, and then things get worse and worse and worse. I think definitely this has to stop. There have been some very good places for runaways here in the Twin Cities —open places where a girl could go and stay. But some changes are taking place that worry me. The current approach seems to be "now that we have been good enough to take you in, we expect you to bare your soul. Tell us all about yourself." That's not what I call an alternative. Neighborhood houses used to offer people refuge, but few such residences exist any more. Desperately needed, I think, is a network of residences all over the country (not only in the cities) where young people can stay for a time and where they will find helping people to talk to if they wish, but only if they wish. These residences might be called youth hostels—not runaway houses or half-way houses. We who work with youth often have gold in our hands, not yet tarnished by the taste of being something bad. Why label prematurely a person in the making? Just because our young people take to the road we don't have to label them runaways.

Changing Structures That Oppress Youth

Q. What can be done politically to change the structures that oppress youth and especially female youth?

G.K. I do not think that youth is totally "oppressed." Perhaps the most important structure in need of change is the family structure where double standards still prevail. Girls in our study often complained that they were not allowed to go out in the evening but their brother was, or the boy was allowed to hike in summer with a group but the girl wasn't. And this distinction was not made on the basis of age; it was strictly boy/girl. Sexuality is not the only basis for uneven treatment, but it certainly is the strongest one.

I see changing the family structure not so much in terms of making a new structure but rather in terms of moving away from the male dominated authoritarian structure. I also see the family structure as a mirror of the political structure. That means in the old monarchies in authoritarian countries the family followed the same pattern. Most people in this country come from this kind of background where the king was at the helm and below him were the people subservient to him. Now it is odd that change in political structure does not necessarily result in change in other structures. It didn't follow in the family; frequently it didn't follow in the schools. But these are structures that need to be changed.

Another structure that definitely must be changed is the one surrounding status offenses. Boys and girls are brought before the courts because they are not going to school. Americans feel very embarrassed because our delinquency figures are so high. Naturally they are when we count every kid that plays truant as a delinquent. I don't know of any other country which does that. If the status offender (the offender who has committed an act that would not be a crime for an adult) were to be taken off the courts, most girls wouldn't even be offenders. Most of the time they are in that category because of "sexual misconduct" which is not considered misconduct among the boys, even today. This will be changed and the change will come through the legal profession. Who will then take care of these girls? Who will work with them? I say it is the responsibility of people in the neighborhoods and of the youth organizations in the community.

Other structures—vocational education, for instance—need to be changed, too. But enough for now.

Reaching Young People

Q. How can we change our approach to young people so that we can reach them?

G.K. They are not so hard to reach. They want to be reached. They want to be listened to; they don't want to be talked down to; and they don't want to be constantly told that they must be exactly what someone else is. I'll finish up with two illuminating poems. The first is one by a 16-year-old girl, written after she was found in the "gutter," labeled "mentally ill," and placed in a mental hospital.

> You aren't normal you know, the fat nurse said accusing
>   me.
> No, I don't know, I said heavily under my breath.
> She heard me though, as her neck stretched out straining to
>   hear more.
> What's your goal in life?
> To castrate all the guys in town and marry the women.
> Not really, just playing a little game.
> She changed the subject because of her uncomfortable posi-
>   tion
> And fixed her gaze steadily upon my poetry book.
> What's your favorite poem?
> I hear America sighing.
> Isn't it, I hear America singing?
> Not the way things are going nowadays, said I, in a flat
>   tone.
> The psychos got up for lunch, and she stood there directing
>   the line.
> I think she felt safer with them.

How little we know about what goes on beneath the hostility we encounter. How fast she catches our fear . . . From another 16-year-old:

I used to be the cocoon all wrapped up
In what I thought then was safety,
Insulating myself from all the hurts and joys of life.
Afraid of so much of love, strangers, of being rejected,
Of trying new things, of being wrong, of being laughed at.
Or of just being.
Snuggled in my security blanket, I miss so much.
Now I am the worm, just breaking through the cocoon
Crawling slowly, inching my way towards the light.
Crawling a little, a little, each day, I hope.
Trying not to slip back a foot for every inch I gain.
Some day I will be that butterfly, free and glorious,
Not afraid of everything I do.

The message I get: Don't make young people feel they have to be afraid; let them be creative; try not to crush the butterfly; let them think, live, be concerned and develop.

RELATED READINGS

Conger, John Janeway. *Adolescence and Youth.* New York: Harper and Row, 1973.
  Related physical development and self concept. Outward appearance and inner self-image are more closely bound together for females than for males.
Gottlieb, David, ed. *Youth in Contemporary Society.* Beverly Hills: Sage Publications, 1973.
  Contributors identify and analyze anticipated trends in youth behavior. Focus is on implications for programs and policies dealing with youth in the decade ahead. Includes good chapter on drugs and one on "the real generation gap."
The Mood of American Youth, 1974. Reston, Virginia: National Association of Secondary School Principals, 1974.

A poll was conducted of 2,000 high school students sampled nationwide by the Gilbert Youth Research Division of Herff-Jones. Outlines the national issues of concern to youth. Reflects a determined and ambitious generation of students who are committed to their own individual goals.

National YWCA Resource Center on Woman. *Teen Women Tell About Their Needs*. New York: National Board, YWCA, 1974.

Questionnaires were sent to 1,111 adolescent women and four workshops were held, to determine young women's concerns. Subject areas are: jobs, sex, recreation, drugs, child care, counseling, racism, women's changing roles. Implications for programs are evident. The project was planned and carried out under the leadership of teen women.

Resource Guide
for Youth Ministry

Michael Warren

The Methodists have been taking a well-organized and intelligent approach to youth ministry for some time. Since they are aware of the important issues in such a ministry, their materials provided countless practical ideas and procedures.

Readings in Youth Ministry

1. Robert L. Browning, "Guidelines for Youth Ministries," 1970.
2. Sheila Campbell, *Your Ministries with Senior Highs*, 1971.
3. Charles Courtoy, "A Guide to Resources: Young Culture," 1973.
4. Charles Courtoy and Clifford Kolb, *Organizing for Youth Ministry*, 1971.
5. John Gattis and James Mayfield, *Your Ministries with Junior Highs*, 1971.
6. Kenneth Mitchell, *Youth Ministry Workbook*, 1969.
7. John Gattis, *et. al.*, "Youth Planbook," 1974-1975.

"Guidelines for Youth Ministries" outlines the role for a youth coordinator in a local Methodist Church. The ten tasks it sets forth for the youth coordinator provide a general summary of the youth ministry approach in a local parish. However, more specific role descriptions and suggestions for programming can be found in *Organizing for Youth Ministry* and the *Youth Ministry Workbook*. Both deserve careful attention by Catholics interested in learning from those who have been giving attention to youth work for many years. The *Workbook* could be adapted and utilized by parish leaders wishing to begin a true ministry to its youth.

The *Your Ministries* books for the senior high and junior high age groups are also quite valuable and could provide the basis for discussion and a sharpening of perspective.

The most valuable aspect in all these materials is the way they combine ministry and education. Their educational preoccupation is with learning, a category that transcends rigid categories of schooling. Further, by putting learning together with ministry, they have emphasized a mission to the total lives of young people. That vision is possibly the one most needed in Catholic parishes.

All the above material is published and available from: Board of Education of the United Methodist Church, Service Department, P.O. Box 871, Nashville, Tennessee 37202.

8. Joan Benson MacDonnell, *There's a Place for You.* Washington: National CYO Federation (1312 Massachusetts Ave., N.W.), 1973, 24 pp., $3.50.

This booklet explores the four roles of a youth worker: educator, enabler, advocate, respondent, attempting thereby to give a clearer focus to youth ministry. It succeeds in presenting an integrated view of parish youth ministry, not limited to schooling or instructional programs. From that point of view, it provides a useful supplement to *To Teach as Jesus Did*, especially the section on youth in the pastoral.

Training Programs for Youth Ministry

1. *Manalive Program*, St. Paul-Minneapolis. The Catholic Youth Centers in St. Paul and in Minneapolis have been active for some time in training programs for youth ministry. Their

Manalive Program, however, goes beyond even their impressive earlier efforts to provide training for young people interested in full-time youth ministry. It is one of the few programs in the country designed to train full-time youth workers for a diocese.

The two Catholic Youth Centers offer a variety of training formats for those interested in working with youth. Their training designs merit study by those wishing to train adults for service to youth. In addition, both centers have programs of service by youth themselves. One such program developed by Father Jim Schuller of the Minneapolis Center is called "On Corps" and involves several weeks of full-time summer service in various public and private institutions in the Twin Cities area.

Information on the unique programs of the two centers can be obtained by writing: (1) Rev. Mike Kolar, St. Paul Catholic Youth Center, 150 North Smith Avenue, St. Paul, Minnesota 55102; (2) Rev. Gerald Trier, Minneapolis Catholic Youth Center, 2120 Park Avenue, Minneapolis, Minnesota 55404.

2. Another training program for full-time youth ministers is currently directed by Don Kimball of Eureka, California. As of last year, Father Kimball had five young people who had agreed to serve in youth ministry for two years at subsistence salaries. His address is: Rev. Don Kimball, Box 999, Eureka, California 95501.

3. A useful program to prepare young people for informal ministry among their peers has been developed recently by Ardyth Hebeisen in Minneapolis in conjunction with the Lutheran-supported Youth Research Center. This program is published as: Ardyth Hebeisen, *Peer Program for Youth* by Augsburg in Minneapolis, 1973. Hebeisen's book is a ten-session group interaction plan for training young people in communication skills. Dealing with ome of the same skills taught in *Parent Effectiveness Training*, this program can help young people understand and actually begin to undertake a ministry of caring among their peers. What the long-range effects of this training may be for developing a wider ministry to youth remains to be seen. However, this program deserves the attention of those working to develop a ministry among the young.

A fascinating report on the background of the Hebeisen

book has been done by Merton Strommen, Director of the Youth Research Center. See Merton Strommen, "Project Youth: Training Youth to Reach Youth," *Character Potential: A Record of Research*, 6:4 (February, 1974), pp. 177-181. Strommen's report underscores the usefulness of a youth-to-youth ministry. (*Character Potential* can be obtained from: Union College Character Research Project, 207 State Street, Schenectady, N.Y. 12305, $4.00 for one volume; single copies $1.50.)

Diocesan Resource Books

Several dioceses have published resource books that may be useful for other dioceses as examples of a way to communicate easily and effectively the variety of resources for youth work within a diocese. Listed below are some recent efforts well worth examining.

1. *The Five P's: People, Places, Programs, Publications, "ph"ilms*. Resources for high school religious education. Archdiocese of St. Paul/Minneapolis, Catholic Education Center, 251 Summit Ave., St. Paul, Minnesota 55102. $2.00

This booklet does just what its title suggests. It provides a listing of resource persons (group leaders, teacher trainers, speakers and their topics), places (youth centers, retreat centers, with complete information about the type of services provided and costs), programs available around the diocese, various publications useful for youth catechesis, and films.

2. *Exchange: A Directory of Some Youth Programs in the Milwaukee Archdiocese*. Office of Religious Education, 345 North 95th St., Milwaukee, Wisconsin 53226.

Exchange appears to be a most valuable resource. It provides rather complete descriptions of a variety of programs being run by various parishes in Milwaukee. The booklet is broken down into the following sections: junior high, confirmation, junior and senior high school, high school CCD, Catholic high school, special programs, index of youth leaders, index of parishes, schools and agencies. The advantage of such a listing is that directors of parish programs can survey descriptions of programs in parishes, identify those similar in philosophy and process to their own, and then get in touch with or visit these programs as a way of exchanging ideas. *Exchange* offers a view of one diocese doing innovative things at the parish level with youth catechesis. This booklet could be used as a model for other dioceses wishing to publish a similar resource booklet.

Another valuable resource available from the Milwaukee CCD Office is the "Thinking of You" page from their monthly newsletter, *Religious Education Tell-Spot*. "Thinking of You," edited by Nancy Hennessey Cooney, describes itself as a resource page for "young adults, their parents, teachers, clergy." Some of the themes of the "Thinking of You" section of the Newsletter have included: Program Planning for Youth (May, 1974); Teens and the Family; Youth and Death; Respect Life: Youth; Respect Life: Elderly; Youth and Ecumenism; and The Adult Friend of Youth. "Thinking of You" is crammed with ideas and also with new and useful resources for those working with the young.

Sister Jane Hurley's booklet, *Are You Searching? Junior High Religious Education Programs in the Archdiocese of St. Paul/Minneapolis*, is quite similar to *Exchange* and just as useful. Written by a long-time leader in junior high catechesis, Sister Hurley's booklet can be obtained from the Catholic Education Center in St. Paul, whose address is listed above.

3. *Diocese of Trenton, Youth Ministries Handbook, 1973*. This loose-leaf filler handbook is a compendium of the services, personnel and programs offered by the various youth service agencies in Trenton, New Jersey. The Handbook is divided into the following sections: Catholic Youth Organization; Parish High School Program; Catholic High School; Other Resources.

Radio/Cassettes

1. Some interesting youth work is currently being done through radio shows aimed at the interests of young people. While formats vary, many tie together several minutes of popu-

lar music, often grouped thematically, followed by interviews
with popular entertainers on various issues youth may be interested in. The religious message of the programs I have heard is
very indirect and low-key.

One denomination offering professionally made cassettes of
songs and interviews are the Methodists. Their *Young Culture
Lifetime* cassettes service (Service Dept., P.O. Box 840, Nashville, Tennessee 37202) is worth investigating by those interested
in launching a youth radio spot for a local area. At the same
address in Nashville, one can order *Music and the Young*, a
monthly newsletter addressed to those interested in reaching the
young through radio and their music ($6.00 per year).

Another contact person is Father Don Kimball of the Diocese of Santa Rosa in California (Box 999, Eureka, Cal. 95501).
Don, who is in charge of youth ministry for his diocese, puts
together weekly radio shows in Eureka that are masterful examples of low-key yet provocative use of radio in ministry to the
young. You can write to him for examples of what he has done.
You may also want to ask him for a copy of his 300 "Fire-
starters" for youth discussion groups and his list of 180 "Suggested Community Awareness/Service Projects."

2. *Quest: The Electronic Journal*, created by Dennis Benson, is a monthly resource for the effective use of media. The
materials center around a cassette but include a newsletter and
printed explanations of some of the exercises and processes explained in the cassette. The special value of *Quest* is as a source
for creative ideas on group process in educational programs for
teens and adults. The cost is judged as reasonable, considering
the expense of producing such materials. For more information,
write *Quest,* Word, Inc., Waco, Texas 76703.

It might be profitable for all concerned if those others who
have worked in radio-for-the-young were in touch with one another to share their ideas and successes.

Liturgical Music

Those interested in liturgical music suited for young people
and in the liturgical formation of young people may find a useful

resource in the new *Folk Mass and Modern Liturgy Magazine.*
Write: Sbuscription Department, P.O. Box 444, Saratoga, California 95070 (published 8 times per year: $8.00).

Other Resources

1. Reverend John E. Forliti, *Program Planner's Manual*,
Catholic Education Center, 251 Summit Ave., St. Paul, Minnesota 55102. This planning manual for youth work, done by the
Director of Religious Education for St. Paul/Minneapolis, is a
valuable resource for those wishing to do serious program planning for young people. In spite of local references, the principles
set forth in this manual will be useful in any diocese of this
country, or of Canada for that matter. The subtitle of John
Forliti's manual captures its special value: "A Planning Model
for the Non-Professional."

2. National Commission on Resources for Youth (36 W.
44th St., New York, N.Y. 10036), is a resource worth being in
contact with. A non-profit, private organization, the Commission seeks to be a resource for those working to develop a sense
of service among youth. Its free quarterly newsletter, *Resources
for Youth*, provides descriptions of youth service programs
around the country. A recent issue focused on peer counseling
programs. The Commission's publication list offers even more
information about various participation projects.

3. The *Network Newsletter and Network Quarterly* (224 D
St., S.E., Washington, D.C. 20003) provides detailed and accurate information on social justice issues, particularly on issues
currently before Congress. For those wishing to keep youth carefully informed about current social justice issues, these publications will be highly prized.

4. *Tool Catalogue* (American Association of University
Women, 2401 Virginia Ave., N.W., Washington, D.C. 20037,
$5.95). The *Tool Catalogue* is a difficult book to describe, so
varied and practical are the ideas it provides. Its subtitle, "Techniques and Strategies for Successful Action Programs," captures
its main thrust. Those wishing to engage young people in various

forms of social action cannot afford to be without this resource. The book is a "how-to" manual, carefully worked out as to action steps and rechecks of those steps to achieve effective social action programs. These "how-to" steps are provided for 59 different social action programs or aspects of programs.